Gandhian Bearings on R.K. Narayan's Novels

Digambar Singh Dewari

ATLANTIC
PUBLISHERS & DISTRIBUTORS (P) LTD

Published by
ATLANTIC
PUBLISHERS & DISTRIBUTORS (P) LTD
7/22, Ansari Road, Darya Ganj,
New Delhi-110002
Phones: +91-11-40775252, 23273880, 23275880, 23280451
Fax: +91-11-23285873
Web: www.atlanticbooks.com
E-mail: orders@atlanticbooks.com

Branch Office
5, Nallathambi Street, Wallajah Road,
Chennai-600002
Phones: +91-44-64611085, 32413319
E-mail: chennai@atlanticbooks.com

ISBN 978-81-269-1464-7

Printed in India at Nice Printing Press, A-33/3A, Site-IV, Industrial Area, Sahibabad, Ghaziabad, U.P.

Acknowledgements

I am deeply grateful to Dr. Rakesh N. Desai, Professor, Department of English, Veer Narmad South Gujarat University, Surat for his invaluable guidance and motivation during this project. To work with him had always been my privilege and pleasure and his innovative ideas and cooperation enabled me to complete this book.

I am thankful to Dr. E.V. Ramakrishnan, Professor and Head of the Department of English, Veer Narmad South Gujarat University, Surat for his constant encouragement. I am grateful to J.N. Pandya, the Principal of Government Arts & Commerce College, Naswadi, for providing me every possible facility to pursue my work. My thanks are due to my colleagues and students for their constant moral support. Further, I express my thanks to the authorities of various libraries across the state for providing me with the required facility.

I also thank my friends, parents, wife and children for imparting such a powerful impetus as could enable me to complete this task. Lastly, thanks are also due to Atlantic Publishers and Distributors (P) Ltd. for evincing interest in publishing this book.

Digambar Singh Dewari

Acknowledgements

Preface

R.K. Narayan is essentially a Gandhian novelist. Gandhian thought, derived largely from Indian tradition which tempered the swoop of nationalism and Western culture with its ingenious practice of truth, non-violence and satyagraha (passive resistance), found morale afresh to the extent that it not only inspired the masses of India, but also opened large avenues for the creative writers to explore.

Notably, Gandhian thought is not a theory in the strict sense of the term as Gandhiji himself once remarked—"there is no ism about it", but a mode based on human values in relation to the exigencies of circumstances. So, the stimulating Gandhian discourse presents different points of view because of its complexity, an average man's inability to understand Gandhi, misuse of Gandhian thought by some crafty people and also due to the experimental truth of Gandhian thought. R.K. Narayan, like a true artist captures this Gandhian sensibility, characterized by the paradigms of Indian and Western cultures, and responds to it imaginatively through his characteristic humour and irony so magnificently that the present study becomes fascinating and rewarding not only for the scholars of Narayan but also for those engaged in Gandhian studies.

Digambar Singh Dewari

Abbreviations

S.A.F.	*Swami and Friends*. 1935; rpt. Mysore: Indian Thought Publications, 2000.
B.O.A.	*The Bachelor of Arts*. 1937; rpt. Mysore: Indian Thought Publications, 1995.
D.R.	*The Dark Room*. 1938; rpt. Mysore: Indian Thought Publications, 1998.
E.T.	*The English Teacher*. 1946; rpt. Mysore: Indian Thought Publications, 1996.
M.S.P.M.	*Mr. Sampath: The Printer of Malgudi*. 1949; rpt. Mysore: Indian Thought Publications, 1998.
F.E.	*The Financial Expert*. 1952; rpt. Mysore: Indian Thought Publications, 1994.
W.F.M.	*Waiting for the Mahatma*. 1955; rpt. Mysore: Indian Thought Publications, 1993.
T.G.	*The Guide*. 1958; rpt. Mysore: Indian Thought Publications, 1995.
M.O.M.	*The Man-Eater of Malgudi*. 1961; rpt. Mysore: Indian Thought Publications, 1994.
V.O.S.	*The Vendor of Sweets*. 1967; rpt. Mysore: Indian Thought Publications, 1992.
P.O.S.	*The Painter of Signs*. 1977; rpt. Mysore: Indian Thought Publications, 1993.
T.M.	*Talkative Man*. 1983; rpt. Mysore: Indian Thought Publications, 1996.

A.T.M.	*A Tiger for Malgudi*. 1986; rpt. Mysore: Indian Thought Publications, 1999.
W.O.N.	*The World of Nagaraj*. 1990; rpt. Mysore: Indian Thought Publications, 1999.
G.T.	*Grandmother's Tale*. 1992; rpt. Mysore: Indian Thought Publications, 2000.

Contents

Introduction: Gandhian Nationalism and R.K. Narayan's Novels

1

The twentieth century Indian literature bears significantly on Gandhian thought. Gandhiji began to influence both national politics and national literature after his return from South Africa in 1915. However, in South Africa Gandhiji had already launched himself as a bold champion of the masses much earlier. His unique ways of dealing with the imperialist government through satyagraha (passive resistance), civil disobedience, love, truth and non-violence fired the imagination of Indians, including the creative writers. Moreover, the other social and political issues advocated by Gandhiji, i.e. education, culture, religion, village-economy, the use of indigenous goods, khaddar and spinning wheel, the boycott of English goods, the rejection of child-marriage, dowry system, untouchability, the advocacy of the cause of women, widow-remarriage, Hindu-Muslim unity, etc. aroused national consciousness and also provided literature with fresh material.

A rapid increase in the sale of *Young India* and *Harijan*, the journals launched by Gandhiji, evidences the wide impact of Gandhian thought all over the country. For example, in 1919 the weekly circulation of *Young India* was less than 2,500 copies, whereas by March 1922 its sale was raised to nearly 40,000 copies per week. Further, the first edition of *An Autobiography or The Story of My Experiments with Truth* in

1927 brought out 6,000 copies. But with the production of 20,000 copies in March 2004 the total number of copies of this book amounted to 10,74,000 copies. Similarly, the thirteenth reprint of Gandhiji's seminal book, *Hind Swaraj or Indian Home Rule* (1938) by February 2000 also testifies a huge impact of Gandhian thought.

Apart from Gandhi's writings, his speech also casts an immense influence on people. Following Gandhian calls, thousands of Indian nationalists, including the creative writers resigned the government jobs to strengthen the movements led by Gandhiji. The creative writers through their writings also undertook to inspire the people to participate in India's struggle for her freedom. Consequently, patriotic feelings increased immensely. India, the nation, became 'Mother India' and she was worshipped like a deity. Similarly, Gandhiji, the saviour of the nation, was also apotheosized as 'father of the nation'. He was also popularly known as 'Bapu' and 'Mahatma' as well.

Considering upon the nation-wide impact of Gandhiji on creative literature, Srinivasa Iyengar terms the period, ranging from the First World War to the end of the Second World War as "the Gandhian Age in India".[1] To quote him further:

> Life could not be the same as before, and every segment of our national life—politics, economics, education, religion, social life, language and literature —acquired a more or less pronounced Gandhian hue. Thus it was that Gandhi exercised a potent influence on our languages and literatures, both directly through his own writings in English and Gujarati and indirectly through the movements generated by his revolutionary thought and practice.[2]

Krishna Kripalani also views that Gandhiji provided "a powerful ethical stimulus to the literary trend" and his "insistence on non-violence and on simplicity and purity in personal life touched a responsive chord in the inherent idealism of Indian thought and thus served as an indirect inspiration to creative literature".[3]

In Indian literature written in Indian languages, Premchand is the representative writer of the Gandhian thought. Inspired by Gandhiji, Premchand resigned the government job on February 14, 1921 and decided to settle in a village to espouse Gandhian thought through his creative writings. Premchand wrote his novels—*Premashrama* (1922), *Rangabhumi* (1925), *Kayakulp* (1926), *Nirmala* (1927), *Gaban* (1931), *Karmabhumi* (1932) and *Godan* (1936), mainly under the influence of Gandhiji. Premchand declares the Gandhian bearings on his novels:

> I think that Mahatma Gandhi is the greatest man in the world. He also aims at the happiness of the labourers and peasants. He is launching movements to promote them. I am encouraging them through my writings. Mahatma Gandhi seeks the Hindu-Muslim unity. I also want to make Hindustani by mixing up Hindi and Urdu.[4]

Thus, Premchand's work pursues and reflects Gandhian thought in letters.

As a national language, Hindi enjoyed a privileged status. Subsequently, of all Indian literature written in Indian languages, Hindi literature shows comparatively a wide impact of Mahatma Gandhi. The poems of Sohan Lal Dwivedi, a Hindi poet, also reveal an immense impact of Gandhiji. Sohan Lal Dwivedi has even dedicated *Bhairevi* (1941), a collection of his poems, to Gandhiji. The Poems in *Bhairevi* include, "Yugavatar Gandhi", "Khadi-Geet", "Gaun Mei", "Jhopariyaun ki Ore", "Kishan", "Dandi-Yatra", "Prarthana (Harijanaun ka Geet)", etc. The poem, "Yugavatar Gandhi" runs as—"Chul pare jidhar do dug mug mai, chul pare koti pug usi ore...." Moreover, the poem ascribes epithets, like "yug parivartak" (reformer of the epoch), "yug sansthapak" (founder of the epoch), "yug sanchalak" (director of the epoch) and "yug nirmata" (maker of the epoch), to Mahatma Gandhi. Thus, the poem magnifies the impact of Gandhiji in poetic terms.

Further, the poems of Sumitranandan Pant, another Hindi poet, also show the impact of Gandhiji in a large measure.

Inspired by Gandhiji's lectures, Sumitranandan Pant bade a farewell to his academic career in 1921, while he was preparing for his intermediate examinations. *Yugpath* (1949), a collection of his poems, includes poems on the theme of Gandhi. Chief among them are "Bapu ke Prati" and "Jai hai, jai Rashtra Pita". Besides, Gandhi figures as one of the major characters in "Lokayatan" (1963), his epic poem.

Apart from these, the works of a majority of Indian writers, writing in Hindi and the vernacular languages of India reflect a vast impact of Gandhiji. Among other writers of note who respond to the impact of Gandhi, as Krishna Kripalani mentions, are "the gifted Gupta brothers, Maithilisharan and Siyaramsharan as well as Jainendra Kumar in Hindi, Kaka Kalelkar and Umashankar Joshi in Gujarati, Mama Warerkar in Marathi, Nilmani Phookan in Assamese, Kalindicharan Panigrahi in Oriya, Annadashankar Ray in Bengali, Bharati in Tamil, Vallathol in Malayalam, and many more in these and other languages".[5]

Like Indian literature written in Indian languages, Indian writings in English also reflect a tremendous influence of Gandhi. Though *Rajmohan's Wife* (1864) by Bankim Chandra Chatterjee claims to be the first Indian novel in English, it was only in the 1930's, i.e. with the maturity of Gandhian thought, that Indian novel in English began to assert itself as a powerful literary mode.

Chief among the Indian novelists in English, writing under the influence of Mahatma Gandhi, are K.S. Venkataramani, Mulk Raj Anand, R.K. Narayan, Raja Rao, Amir Ali, Ahmad Abbas, Nayantara Sahgal and K. Nagarajan.

K.S. Venkataramani's *Murgan the Tiller* (1927) champions the economic theory of Mahatma Gandhi and *Kandan the Patriot: A Novel of New India in the Making* (1932) reflects the Gandhian political thoughts.

Similarly, Gandhian philosophy exercises an immense influence on Mulk Raj Anand. A true follower of Gandhi's political thoughts, Mulk Raj Anand participated in the Civil Disobedience Campaign of 1921 and was imprisoned for a day. Moreover, inspired by an article in *Young India* by

Gandhiji, describing Gandhi's love for Uka, a sweeper boy, Mulk Raj Anand came back to Ahmedabad from London and revised the manuscript of his first novel, *Untouchable* (1935), as advised by Gandhiji for "three months in the Sabarmati Ashram".[6]

Alike his contemporaries, R.K. Narayan (1906-2001) is also influenced by Mahatma Gandhi. All of his novels, right from *Swami and Friends* (1935) to *Grandmother's Tale* (1992), reveal a powerful impact of Gandhian philosophy. But *Waiting for the Mahatma* (1955) and *The Vendor of Sweets* (1967) relate more significantly to the ideals of Gandhiji.

Raja Rao's *Kanthapura* (1938) portrays the impact of Mahatma Gandhi perhaps more vividly than any other Indian novel in English. M.K. Naik observes *Kanthapura* as "the finest evocation of the Gandhian age in Indian English fiction".[7] Not only Raja Rao's literary writings but his personal life also reflects the impact of Gandhian philosophy. Few years after the publication of *Kanthapura*, Raja Rao visited Mahatma Gandhi at Sevagram in his quest for self-realization. He also participated in the Quit India Movement of 1942.

Further, Amir Ali's novel, *Conflict* (1947) revolves around the Quit India Movement of 1942, launched by Mahatma Gandhi. Similarly, *Inqilab* (1955) by Ahmad Abbas is imbued with the political thoughts of Mahatma Gandhi. The novel gives an account of the political upheavals, including the Rowlatt Bill, the Jallianwala Bagh massacre, the Salt Satyagraha and the Gandhi-Irwin Pact of 1931.

The influence of Mahatma Gandhi on the works of Nayantara Sahgal is even more pronounced. B.P. Sinha rightly points out: "The Gandhian values have formed the basis of Sahgal's approach to problems, both political and personal."[8] Nayantara Sahgal's first novel *A Time to be Happy* (1957) describes the Congress activities and the Quit India Movement of 1942. Similarly, K. Nagarajan's *Chronicles of Kedaram* (1961) elaborates on some of the major Gandhian issues, like untouchability, Hindu-Muslim unity, conflict between the East and the West, the haves and have-nots. Moreover, the novel also introduces Mahatma Gandhi engaged in uniting two families.

The present study intends to examine critically the impact of Mahatma Gandhi's ideas on R.K. Narayan's novels. Unlike Mulk Raj Anand and Raja Rao, R.K. Narayan does not seem to have personal contacts with Mahatma Gandhi. Nor did R.K. Narayan ever take part in any of the Gandhian movements. Moreover, the volumes of *Akshardeh* published in Gujarati do not indicate any correspondence between Gandhi and R.K. Narayan. But Narayan did respond to Indian reality coloured by Gandhian thoughts. To quote Rama Jha:

> Moreover, the Gandhian movement was not only a political movement. It was a movement that, for the first time in Indian history, generated and raised social issues. The ferment that Gandhian thought created, encompassed the whole social milieu and touched on issues that affected man as a whole in various facets and stages of life. More importantly, it made Indian men and women aware of themselves. It is this sense of awareness that revolutionized Indians and made them seek their national as also their individual identity. It is Gandhian thought that brought the colonial encounter to the fore. It is in this social situation created by Gandhian thought that Narayan like other contemporary novelists, found his subject matter.[9]

As a creative writer R.K. Narayan also sensed the catalytic effect of Gandhi and registered it in his fiction.

Even a cursory reading of R.K. Narayan's novels evidences the Gandhian influence on them. The two of R.K. Narayan's novels, namely *Waiting for the Mahatma* (1955) and *The Vendor of Sweets* (1967), are based on the Myth of Gandhi. Narayan's novels refer to Mahatma Gandhi arbitrarily through various titles, i.e. "Gandhi", "Gandhiji", "Mahatma", "Mahatmaji", "Mahatma Gandhi" and also as "Bapu" and "Bapuji". And this Gandhi title recurs frequently in a majority of Narayan's novels. For example, Gandhiji's name recurs nine times in *Talkative Man* (1983), seven times in *Swami and*

Friends (1935), six times in *The Man-Eater of Malgudi* (1961), five times each in *Mr. Sampath: The Printer of Malgudi* (1949) and *The Painter of Signs* (1977), four times in *The Guide* (1958), three times both in *The Financial Expert* (1952) and *The World of Nagaraj* (1990), and once in *A Tiger for Malgudi* (1986).

However, a few of R.K. Narayan's novels—*The Bachelor of Arts* (1937), *The Dark Room* (1938), *The English Teacher* (1946) and *Grandmother's Tale* (1992) do not refer directly to Gandhi. But they also, like his other novels, seem to embody the Gandhian philosophy. Moreover, *The Bachelor of Arts* refers to the Civil Disobedience Movement, led by Gandhiji.

Thus, R.K. Narayan presents Gandhian philosophy in his novels. Michel Pousse supports this view:

> Narayan penetrated the heart of Gandhi's teaching. He separated the obviously ephemeral implications of his philosophy from what was eternal in it and he gave literary existence to the latter.[10]

Besides, the Gandhian bearings on R.K. Narayan's novels can be traced at a deeper level, in terms of a perspective, a scale of basic values, a vision of life. Rama Jha aptly remarks:

> The influence of Gandhian thought is incorporated in the vision of life that Narayan's novels present. His novels uphold traditional Indian values, but, these are not the values of ancient Indian tradition, but values reoriented by Gandhian thought. Narayan's novels, right from his first, *Swami and Friends* (1935) to *The Vendor of Sweets* (1967) and even *The Painter of Signs* (1977) unmistakably highlight and endorse Gandhian philosophy.[11]

It may be useful to probe further Gandhian ideas in the context of Indian nationalism. Prior to the emergence of Mahatma Gandhi as a national leader, national consciousness with its ardent spirits of patriotism and liberty had rapidly begun to unite the entire nation. The Indian Mutiny of 1857 gave the Indians a big opportunity to think of India as one nation. Apart from newspapers, the creative and non-creative writings also served to strengthen the national consciousness among Indians. Bankim Chandra Chatterjee's song "Bande Mataram" (Hail to thee, Mother) from his novel, *Anandamath* (1882) became a hymn and slogan of Indian nationalists in their struggle for independence. Rabindranath Tagore's *Gitanjali* (1912) also inspired Indians to imbibe the feelings of patriotism and pride. Similarly, Muhammad Iqbal's famous song "Sare Jahan Se Achha Hindustan Hamara" (Our India is the best in the world) glorified India as a distinct nation.

Among the non-literary writings V.D. Savarkar's *The Indian War of Independence—1857* (1909) is perhaps the foremost book that enabled the rise of Indian nationalism. Originally written in Marathi, the book presents a historical account of the revolt of 1857 in India from the Indian point of view. But the book was proscribed before it could be published in any Indian press. However, the revolutionary group active in Europe managed its printing in Holland in 1909 and dispatched its copies to India, America and Japan, wrapped in artistic covers bearing bogus titles like "Pickwick Papers", "Scott's Works" or "Don Quixote". Everywhere the book was read with a great interest and it became the Bible of the Indian revolutionists.

In 18th century nationalism erupted as a dominant movement in Western Europe and North America. However, it reached India much later, i.e. in the beginning of 20th century. John Plamenatz classifies nationalism into two types—"western" and "eastern".[12] By Western nationalism he does mean the nationalism that sprang in Western Europe, and the Eastern nationalism is the nationalism that prevailed in Africa, Asia and also in Latin America.

Thus, Gandhi's emergence on the Indian political scene is hailed by Indian nationalism, characterized by patriotism and liberty. Besides, the advent of Western nationalism in the Indian subcontinent did also cast a strong spell on Indian nationalism. Moreover, the overpowering sweep of nationalism accorded issues like 'nation' and 'nationalism' a central position in such a nationalist discourse. Further, nation and nationalism were defined variously by both the Eastern and the

Western nationalists. For example, Dr. Radhakrishnan views nation as "a spiritual possession".[13] Similarly, Homi K. Bhabha defines nation as "one of the major structures of ideological ambivalence within the cultural representations of modernity".[14] And Ernest Renan defines nation as "a soul, a spiritual principle".[15]

Similarly, John Bowle defines nationalism as an expression of a "healthy solidarity, the love of hearth and home and family; a proper pride in a native culture".[16] Further, Jonathan Friedman remarks that nationalism implies "the establishment of a culturally distinct nation state society that is essentially identical to other such state societies except for its ethnic distinctiveness".[17] Similarly, Benedict Anderson argues that "nationalism has to be understood by aligning it, not with self-consciously held political ideologies, but with the large cultural systems that preceded it, out of which—as well as against which—it came into being".[18] Further, John Plamenatz argues that nationalism is "the desire to preserve or enhance a people's national or cultural identity when that identity is threatened, or the desire to transform or even create it where it is felt to be inadequate or lacking".[19] And Ashis Nandy holds that nationalism is a "rebellion against the West on the political plane".[20]

In view of these definitions of nationalism, it can be argued that Gandhian nationalism is neither a slavish imitation of Western nationalism, nor can it ignore Western nationalism completely. Partha Chatterjee comments:

> The 'Eastern' type of nationalism, consequently, has been accompanied by an effort to 're-equip' the nation culturally, to transform it. But it could not do so simply by imitating the alien culture, for then the nation would lose its distinctive identity. The search, therefore, was for a regeneration of the national culture, adapted to the requirements of progress, but retaining at the same time its distinctiveness.[21]

Thus, Gandhian nationalism seeks to rebuild the nation in the light of her ancient glory and also the ideals of liberty, equality and liberality, characterized by Western nationalism.

Obviously, at the political level, Gandhian nationalism seeks the overthrow of the British rule from India. At the social level, it presents a quest for the upliftment of women, the downtrodden and the eradication of untouchability. At the economic level, it seeks to promote khadi and other village industries and also condemns the use of machinery. At the educational level, it discards English education and advocates national education scheme. And at the cultural level, it is a sincere appeal to the Indian nationalists to imbibe their rich cultural heritage and also to eschew the materialistic, immoral and irreligious civilization of the West.

So, culture acquires a pivotal position in a nationalist discourse. And like nation and nationalism, culture is also defined variously. Edward B. Tylor defines culture as "that complex whole which includes knowledge, belief, art, morals, law, custom, and any other capabilities and habits acquired by man as a member of society".[22] Clyde Kluckhohn views culture as a "kind of learned behavior, which, in its specific aspects, is common to a group of people, transmitted by the older generation to its offspring, or transmitted in some portion by any member of one group to a member or members of another group".[23] Gandhiji defines culture as a "part of the web and woof of everyday life".[24] Further, Dr. S. Radhakrishnan defines culture as "the quality of mind" which a man "brings to bear on the facts of life".[25]

Though some anthropologists deny any difference between culture and civilization, they differ a little at the conceptual level. The former is an abstract phenomenon and traces the progress of inner faculties in a man, whereas the latter records the material progress of man in terms of science and technology.

Quite interestingly, the European culture in India greatly lured Indians on the one hand and on the other it enormously became critical among Indians. Rabindranath Tagore points out the heterogeneity of European culture:

> ...the perennial centre of European culture is sure to be in Europe. And therefore, if we must accept it as the only source of light for our mind, then it would be

> like depending upon some star for our daybreak, which is the sun of a far distant alien sphere. The star may give us light, but not the day; it may give us direction in our voyage of exploration, but it can never open the full view of truth before our eyes. In fact, we can never use this star light for stirring sap in our invisible depth and giving colour and bloom to our life.[26]

Similarly, Swami Vivekananda advises Indians to eschew European culture:

> In the first place, we cannot become Westerns; therefore, imitating the Westerns is useless. Suppose you can imitate the Westerns, that moment you will die, you will have no more life in you. In the second place, it is impossible. A stream is taking its rise, away beyond where time began, flowing through millions of ages of human history; do you mean to get hold of that stream, and push it back to its source, to a Himalayan glacier? Even if that were practicable, it would not be possible for you to be Europeanised. If you find it is impossible for the European to throw-off the few centuries of culture which there is in the West, do you think it is possible for you to throw-off the culture of shining scores of centuries? It cannot be.[27]

Thus, culture marks a national heritage.

Further, B.P. Singh, a historian, also points out the unique features of Indian culture:

> India's culture which blossomed more than 3000 years ago, has given successive generations of Indians a mind-set, a value system, and a way of life, which has been retained with remarkable continuity despite the passage of time, repeated foreign invasions, and the enormous growth in population.[28]

Similarly, Gandhiji also comments on the rich cultural heritage of India: "It is my firm opinion, that no culture has treasures so rich as ours has."[29]

Gandhian ideas, in the nationalist discourse, incorporate Indian culture in terms of identity as well as modernity. R.K. Narayan's novels largely seem to espouse the Gandhian ideas in this context. *The Dark Room*, *Mr. Sampath: The Printer of Malgudi*, *The Guide*, *The Man-Eater of Malgudi*, *The Vendor of Sweets* seem to criticize the immoral ways of Western civilization from the Gandhian viewpoint. Besides, *Swami and Friends*, *Mr. Sampath: The Printer of Malgudi*, *The Guide* and *The Painter of Signs* also mark the religious degeneration. Moreover, *The Financial Expert*, *The Guide*, *The Man-Eater of Malgudi* and *The Vendor of Sweets* not only expatiate on the over-materialistic tendency of Western civilization but also prove its evil consequences as envisaged by Gandhiji.

The Gandhian dislike for English education casts its shadow mainly on *Swami and Friends, The Bachelor of Arts, The English Teacher, The Financial Expert, The Guide* and *The Vendor of Sweets.* Similarly, *Waiting for the Mahatma, The Man-Eater of Malgudi, The Vendor of Sweets* and *A Tiger for Malgudi* seem to espouse Gandhian non-violence. Further, *Waiting for the Mahatma* and *The Vendor of Sweets* interpret the Gandhian advocacy of khadi and tanning. And the Gandhian love for human beings and animals echoes quite often in a majority of Narayan's novels.

The Dark Room, *The Guide* and *The Painter of Signs* espouse the Gandhian cause of women. And the Gandhian concern for child-marriage, dowry system, caste and untouchability also echo in a majority of Narayan's novels. Further, village, which draws Gandhiji's attention the most, also explains itself through the portrayal of Malgudi and the surrounding villages.

Thus, the term 'Gandhian' refers to a specific period in national history (roughly from 1914 to 1950) which marks a deep influence of Gandhian thought on creative writing. Besides, 'Gandhian' may also be used to denote recognition of that thought in terms of a mode popularized as 'Gandhism'. However, Gandhi denies any 'ism' to his philosophy. To quote Gandhiji:

> Well, all my philosophy, if it may be called by that pretentious name, is contained in what I have said. You will not call it 'Gandhism': there is no ism about it.[30]

Ironically, Gandhism which influenced creative literature so enormously over a long period, itself lacks consistency. Gandhiji himself confesses:

> At the time of writing I never think of what I have said before. My aim is not to be consistent with my previous statements on a given question, but to be consistent with truth as it may present itself to me at a given moment.[31]

In a similar way, the term 'bearing' may be used to determine the extent of Gandhi available to Narayan's fiction. Narayan may present Gandhi directly. And he may also present Gandhi through the points of view of people around him. As Shakti Batra observes:

> The best thing for the contemporary novelist would be to keep Gandhi in the background but make his influence felt indirectly. This is what Narayan has done.[32]

In other words, Narayan may deal with different representations of Gandhi by employing his various fictional techniques, such as irony and humour.

Obviously, the latter mode of presenting Gandhi may lead to different versions of Gandhi. For instance, in *Waiting for the Mahatma* Narayan seems to laugh at Sriram who joins Bharati, a young girl devoted to the cause of Gandhi, not out of his faith in Gandhi, but due to his fascination for her. Similarly, in *The Vendor of Sweets* Jagan's very portrayal as a follower of Gandhi, yet his greed for wealth, prompting Jagan to avoid tax and take his cheque book even to the forest in his final retreat, are ironic and also hint at people's failure to understand Gandhi thoroughly.

The present study proposes to relate Gandhian nationalism to R.K. Narayan's novels. So, a recourse will be made to the relevant literature in Gandhian studies. An attempt will also be made to find out the way Narayan's creative genius has sensed Gandhian ideas in his fiction through characteristic mode of irony and humour.

NOTES

1. K.R.S. Iyengar, *Indian Writing in English* (1984; rpt. New Delhi: Sterling Publishers Pvt. Ltd., 2005), p. 248.
2. *Ibid.*, pp. 248-49.
3. Krishna Kripalani, "Modern Literature" in *A Cultural History of India*, ed. A.L. Basham (Oxford: Clarendon Press, 1975), pp. 406-22.
4. Shivrani Devi Premchand, *Premchand Ghar Mei* (Delhi: Atmaram & Sons, 1991), p. 95. (Translated from Hindi the relevant portion by me.)
5. Krishna Kripalani, *op. cit.*, pp. 406-22.
6. Mulk Raj Anand, "Why I Write?" in *Perspectives on Mulk Raj Anand*, ed. K.K. Sharma (Ghaziabad: Vimal Prakashan, 1978), pp. 1-8.
7. M.K. Naik, *Dimensions of Indian English Literature* (New Delhi: Sterling Publishers Pvt. Ltd., 1984), p. 105.
8. B.P. Sinha, *Social and Political Concern in the Novels of Nayantara Sahgal* (Jaipur: Book Enclave, 2001), p. 29.
9. Rama Jha, *Gandhian Thought and Indo-Anglian Novelists* (Delhi: Chanakya Publications, 1983), pp. 119-20.
10. Michel Pousse, "R.K. Narayan as a Gandhian Novelist", *The Literary Criterion*, XXV, No. 4 (1990), pp. 77-90.
11. Rama Jha, *op. cit.*, pp. 46-47.
12. John Plamenatz, "Two Types of Nationalism" in *Nationalism: The Nature and Evolution of an Idea*, ed. Eugene Kamenka (London: Edward Arnold Ltd., 1976), pp. 22-36.
13. S. Radhakrishnan, *Freedom and Culture* (Madras: G. A. Natesan & Co., 1936), p. 37.
14. Homi K. Bhabha, "Introduction: Narrating the Nation" in *Nation and Narration*, ed. Homi K. Bhabha (London: Routledge, 1990), pp. 1-7.
15. Ernest Renan, "What is a Nation?" in *Nation and Narration*, ed. Homi K. Bhabha (London: Routledge, 1990), pp. 8-22.
16. John Bowle, *The Nationalist Idea* (London: Ampersand Ltd., 1955), p. 9.
17. Jonathan Friedman, *Cultural Identity and Global Process* (London: Sage Publications, 1994), p. 87.
18. Benedict Anderson, *Imagined Communities: Reflections on the Origin and Spread of Nationalism* (1983; rpt. London: Verso, 1991), p. 12.
19. John Plamenatz, *op. cit.*
20. Ashis Nandy, *The Illegitimacy of Nationalism: Rabindranath Tagore and the Politics of Self* (Delhi: Oxford University Press, 1994), p. 89.

21. Partha Chatterjee, *Nationalist Thought and the Colonial World: A Derivative Discourse*? (Delhi: Oxford University Press, 1986), p. 2.
22. Edward B. Tylor, *Primitive Culture: Researches into the Development of Mythology, Philosophy, Religion, Language, Art and Custom,* Vol. I (London: Garden City Press Ltd., 1913), p. 1.
23. Clyde Kluckhohn, *Culture and Behavior* (1962; rpt. New York: The Free Press of Glencoe, 1964), pp. 22-23.
24. K.G. Saiyidain, *Significance of Gandhi as a Man and Thinker* (1970; rpt. New Delhi: Publications Division, Ministry of Information and Broadcasting, Govt. of India, 1994), p. 59.
25. S. Radhakrishnan, *op. cit.*, p. 30.
26. Rabindranath Tagore, *The Centre of Indian Culture* (Madras: The Society for the Promotion of National Education, 1919) p. 37.
27. Swami Vivekananda, *The Complete Works of Swami Vivekananda*, Vol. III (Almora: Advaita Ashram, 1932), p. 172.
28. B.P. Singh, *India's Culture: The State, the Arts and Beyond* (New Delhi: Oxford University Press, 1998), p. 1.
29. M.K. Gandhi, "National Education", *Young India*, III, No. 35 (September 1, 1921), pp. 276-77.
30. Mahadev Desai, "Weekly Letters", *Harijan*, IV, No. 7 (March 28, 1936), pp. 49-51.
31. M.K. Gandhi, "Conundrums", *Harijan*, VII, No. 34 (September 30, 1939), pp. 288-89.
32. Shakti Batra, "Impact of Gandhi on Indian Writing", *Indian Literature*, XVII, No. 3 (1974), pp. 38-51.

Education: The Quest for Identity in Gandhi and Narayan

2

Ordinarily, education means a knowledge of letters. But education is a wide term which involves a proper training of both the mind and body. Swami Vivekananda considers education as a "development of faculty".[1] And Gandhiji himself defines education as "an all-round drawing out of the best in child and man—body, mind and spirit".[2]

Like other vital issues, education also draws remarkably Gandhiji's attention. Both, in his speeches and writings, Gandhiji criticizes British education, primarily on three grounds—(i) it is based on foreign culture, (ii) it fails to cater to the all-round development of a child, (iii) it is inimical to the growth of vernacular languages and literatures of India. Therefore, Gandhiji stresses the need for a national scheme of education.

In his books *Basic Education* (1951), *Towards New Education* (1953) and *The Problem of Education* (1962), Gandhiji condemns the British education and advocates a national scheme of education. Besides, the chapters of *India of My Dreams* (1947)—"Evil Wrought by the Foreign Medium", "The New Education", "Basic Education", "Higher Education", "Ashram Ideal of Education", and "Women's Education" elaborate on the issue of education. Further, "On Education" (XVIIth Chapter) of *Selections from Gandhi* (1948), edited by Nirmal Kumar Bose points out the defects of

British education system. Similarly, the articles—"Criticism Answered" (*Harijan* Vol. V, No. 25) and "Higher Education" (*Harijan* Vol. VI, No. 22) also bring out Gandhi's ideal of education. Moreover, the article "Gandhi and Value Education" by Ranjit Chaudhuri, which appeared in the issue of *Gandhi Marg* (April-June 1994), a renowned journal on Gandhian studies, also throws light on the objectives of Gandhian education.

Therefore, Gandhiji is thoroughly against the British education in India. To quote him:

> It is worth noting that, by receiving English education, we have enslaved the nation. Hypocrisy, tyranny, etc. have increased; English-knowing Indians have not hesitated to cheat and strike terror into the people.[3]

But the Gandhian scheme of education is not merely a criticism of English education. Nor does it virtually discard the teaching of English literature in India. Gandhiji himself confesses that he has a great love for English and its noble literature. Besides, he recommends the teaching of English literature to Indians through translation of English texts into Indian languages.

Nor does the Gandhian education simply copy the ancient Gurukul system of education. For instance, in his scheme of education, Gandhiji imbibes the Gurukul ideal of the teacher-taught relation. But simultaneously, he did not believe in the rigorous training which a child had to undergo under the Gurukul system. Instead, he suggests that the child should learn naturally without exerting any rigour. Next, under the Gurukul system a child had to compulsorily undergo physical activities in the form of a routine work, i.e. cleanliness of the ashram and its surroundings, fetching water, cutting firewoods, rearing cattle, etc. However, in his scheme of education, Gandhiji also reserves a provision for physical activities. He advocates education through vocational crafts in order to make education self-supporting. D.S. Sarma sums up the motto of Gandhian education: "And on the educational side his program provided for a new system of education which centered round a craft and which insisted on the cultivation of both the mother tongue and a national language common to all India."[4]

Hence, Gandhian scheme of education provides an alternative system of education. It is distinct both from the Gurukul system and the English education. In other words, it seeks to interpret the ideals of the Gurukul in terms of modern Indian reality. Moreover, it also allows to incorporate English education only if English education tends to promote, directly or indirectly, the linguistic, literary and cultural values of India. Therefore, the Gandhian scheme of education is termed as 'national education'. It is applied both to the basic and higher education.

Thus, education in contemporary India emerges as an identity asserting itself as a mode rather than a convention. This identity embraces a variety with its threefold mission—reinterpretation of ancient educational values in the present context, enabling educational institutions to obtain self-sufficiency through crafts, and also incorporating the tenets of English education only if they tend to contribute to the growth of Indian vernaculars and literatures.

There emerge a few significant components of the Gandhian education, enumerated as under:

1. Immature quest for education in the contemporary society
2. Women's liberation through education
3. English education as an imperialist strategy
4. The British examination system
5. National education.

In view of the first component, immature quest for education in the contemporary society, it is necessary to argue here that the existing system of education greatly pained Gandhiji. He bravely points out that the existing system of education is completely devoid of a true meaning, aim or objective. Ironically, this system of education, despite its severe criticism by Indian nationalists, created a spell among Indians. In fact, the British education system, introduced in 1835, brought about an upsurge of education in India. Earlier, the educational set up of India was largely controlled and monopolized by the upper class people, i.e. the Brahmins, the Mullas and the Moulvis. Besides, women's education was also discouraged.

But the British education system made education open to all, irrespective of caste, creed or gender. Naturally, these factors contributed to the spread of education in India. Further, the tendency among Indians to consider government jobs superior to vocational crafts, diverted young boys and girls from the crafts to education. It also led to a sudden increase in the number of students in schools and colleges. Chittaranjan Das aptly comments on the spell created by education: "We turn out B.A.'s and M.A.'s by the thousand from the University mills just as buttons and pin-heads may be turned out in English factories."[5] Gandhiji also notes the craze for education among Indians. But he also regrets the inability of the people to understand the true meaning of education:

> The word Education is very much in use these days; almost everybody has something to say about it. The schools—whether Government or private—are packed with students. So are the colleges. A number of students seeking admission to the Gujarat College had to go back disappointed. But despite this increasing desire for education hardly anyone ponders as to what education really is.[6]

Quite in conformity with this Gandhian viewpoint, R.K. Narayan's novels register a keen awareness of education. N. Ranganath rightly observes: "Narayan never forgets to allot considerable space for discussing the eternal problem—the system of education in India."[7] A majority of R.K. Narayan's novels namely, *Swami and Friends*, *The Bachelor of Arts*, *The Dark Room*, *The English Teacher*, *The Financial Expert*, *The Guide*, *The Vendor of Sweets* and *The World of Nagaraj*, deal with the issue of education, characteristically in a Gandhian way.

R.K. Narayan's novels lay stress on education to the extent that it is essential for a child to attend his school everyday under all circumstances from the father's point of view. For instance, in *Swami and Friends* Swaminathan, displeased at his father's insistence to send him to school against his desire on a particular day, whispers into his granny's ear, "Granny, even if I die, I am sure father will insist on sending my corpse to the school" (*S.A.F.*, p. 131). And at school Swaminathan's headmaster insults and punishes Swaminathan for his absence from Drill and Scouting classes. The headmaster further warns: "And remember W.S. Swaminathan, if you miss a single class again, I shall strip you in the school hall and ask the peon to cane you" (*S.A.F.*, p. 144). It is perhaps due to the excessive emphasis on education that Donald Barr views *Swami and Friends* as a "beguiling comedy of a Hindu schoolboy".[8]

Further, in *The Dark Room* also Ramani makes it a point to send his son to school everyday against all odds. Unmoved by his wife's pleadings, Ramani makes it clear to his son, saying: "Don't miss your school on any account" (*D.R.*, p. 1). Further, Jagan in *The Vendor of Sweets* appeals to Mali, his son, not to leave his college half way through. And when Jagan finds himself unable to change Mali's mind, Jagan requests his cousin to persuade Mali to continue with his education.

Besides, in *The Financial Expert*, the Schooling Ceremony of Balu, Margayya's son, lends a strong support to the spell created by education:

> When Balu was six years old Margayya admitted him to the Town Elementary School. Margayya made a great performance of it. He took the young man in a decorated motor with pipes and drums through the Market Road: the traffic was held up for half an hour when Balu's procession passed. Balu sat with the top of his head shaved, with diamonds sparkling on his ear lobes, and a rose garland round his neck, in a taxi with four of his picked friends by his side. Margayya walked in front of the car, and he had invited a few citizens of the road to go with him as well. (*F.E.*, pp. 105-06)

Although the portrayal of Balu's Schooling Ceremony bears a tinge of satire, it fictionally interprets the historical zeal for education among people as mentioned by Gandhiji.

The stress on education makes education quite a sensitive issue. It determines relationship among individuals. In *The Financial Expert* the cause of Balu's education prompts Margayya's brother to shy away his ill-will against Margayya, thereby enabling him to participate in Balu's Schooling Ceremony. Similarly, in *The Vendor of Sweets* Jagan's insistence on his son's resuming his education confronts the latter's apathy to education. Consequently, the father-son relationship receives a heavy blow. Jagan remarks: "He had never suspected that his zeal for education was going to ruin their relationship" (*V.O.S.*, p. 33). And in *The World of Nagaraj*, Nagaraj's proposal to admit Tim, Gopu's son, to a school when Tim is five years old, pleases Gopu, quite against Nagaraj's expectation. But later, Tim's rejection of his education halfway through and Nagaraj's attempt to defend Tim incur Gopu's wrath. Rita Joshi observes:

> Nagaraj, the antihero of the novel, issueless and a younger son, placidly watches life pass by from his corner of Kabir Street. But his nephew Tim's antics disturb his calm and he is forced to venture into the world. His dismay at Tim's activities conflicts with his protective avuncular feelings, and in trying to be supportive of Tim's dropping out of school and his subsequent alcoholic escapades at Kismet, the local bar, he earns his brother Gopu's wrath.[9]

Nagaraj also marks that his negligence over Tim's education has also caused a breach between himself and Professor Jesudoss.

Thus, the excessive zeal for a child's education in Narayan's novels, and the portrayal of Balu's Schooling Ceremony in *The Financial Expert* reflect the spread of education in Indian society, as noted by Gandhiji.

Besides, Narayan's novels accord a distinct status to education. In *The Financial Expert,* the blanket seller has "evidently great reverence for learned people" (*F.E.*, p. 129). Similarly, Sriram in *Waiting for the Mahatma* believes that a man with higher education is endowed with necessary polish. Sriram reflects: "That was why it was urged on him to go to a college and pass his B.A." (*W.F.M.*, p. 24). In *The Guide* Raju as a young boy would mark his father bragging before others that "his son was going to a school" (*T.G.*, p. 25). And in *The Man-Eater of Malgudi* Nataraj pampers his little school-going son with toys, books, sweets and many other things.

Consequently, the awareness of education increases to the extent that education is regarded as indispensable. In *The Guide* when Raju learns that the people of village Mangala prefer to send their children out to graze their cattle rather than sending them to a school, he explains to the villagers:

> Boys must read, first. They must, of course, help their parents, but they must also find the time to study. (*T.G.*, p. 44)

Similarly, in *The World of Nagaraj* Professor Jesudoss asserts: "All very well, but education should come first" (*W.O.N.*, p. 75). Further, Saroja's father insists that Saroja "must complete her M.A. first" (*W.O.N.*, p. 91). Moreover, education becomes the most discussed of all the issues. Mali's cousin in *The Vendor of Sweets* remarks: "You could always hit education if you had no other target" (*V.O.S.*, p. 27).

Moreover, some of the characters seem to develop a great faith in education. For example, Margayya in *The Financial Expert* is led to believe that if he does not put his child to school he will soon turn out to be "a terrible scoundrel" (*F.E.*, p. 53). Similarly, in *The Guide* Raju's father also believes that education alone may prevent Raju from picking up bad words any more.

Most of the protagonists in Narayan's novels are highly educated. Chandran in *The Bachelor of Arts*, Shanta Bai in *The Dark Room*, Grace in *The Vendor of Sweets*, Daisy in *The Painter of Signs*, Nagaraj, Gopu and Saroja in *The World of Nagaraj*, are all graduates. Moreover, Gopu is a B.A. with first class. Jagan in *The Vendor of Sweets* considers graduation as the basic qualification. And Krishnan in *The English Teacher* is a lecturer in Albert Mission College. Further, *Mr. Sampath: The Printer of Malgudi* points out that it is a tradition of Srinivas and his family to graduate themselves at Malgudi in the Albert Mission College and thereafter move on to Madras for higher studies in law.

Further, Rosie in *The Guide* is an M.A. in Economics and Macro, her husband, is a man of academic interests. Even Vasu, a taxidermist, in *The Man-Eater of Malgudi* is an M.A. in History, Economics and Literature. Similarly, in *The Painter of Signs* Raman, a signboard painter, has also received his college education. However, the upsurge of education gets reflected in *The Dark Room* through Ramani:

> We struggle hard, get our B.A., and think that we are the first of our kind; but what happens? We find that there are thousands like us. (*D.R.*, p. 67)

But those who fail to obtain a university degree do regret afterwards. Ramani in *The Dark Room* "occasionally longed for a degree" (*D.R.*, p. 140). Besides, Jagan in *The Vendor of Sweets* nostalgically craves: "If I had passed the B.A., I could have done so many other things" (*V.O.S.*, p. 27).

Such a boundless quest for education in Narayan's novels leads a number of characters to engage themselves in literary or quasi-literary pursuits. Srinivas in *Mr. Sampath: The Printer of Malgudi* edits *The Banner*, a weekly paper. Dr. Pal in *The Financial Expert* claims to have written a book, *Domestic Harmony*. Marco in *The Guide* publishes a book entitled, *The Cultural History of South India*. Nataraj's friend, a poet, in *The Man-Eater of Malgudi*, is engaged in writing an epic narrating the life of Lord Krishna in monosyllabic verse. And Vasu persuades Nataraj to print the forest officer's book entitled *Golden Thoughts*. Besides, Jagan in *The Vendor of Sweets* frequently inquires from his printer about the printing of his magnum opus on *Nature Cure and Natural Diet*. And in *The World of Nagaraj*, Nagaraj strains every nerve to fulfil his grandiloquent desire to write the life of Sage Narada.

Like the onrush of students in educational institutions as described by Gandhiji, R.K. Narayan's novels also display the schools and colleges teeming with students. Even the eccentric headmaster's private school for small children in *The English Teacher* has "over two hundred pupils" (*E.T.*, p. 177). Krishnan in Albert Mission College teaches "a thousand boys"

(*E.T.*, p. 26). However, *The Guide* hints at the onrush of students in schools and colleges. Raju from his book-stall at the railway station notes that "the train brought in more and more school-going population, and the 10.30 local train was full of young men going off to Albert Mission College" (*T.G.*, p. 48). Moreover, *The Bachelor of Arts* also presents the overcrowded vision of a classroom. Mr. Gajapathi, the Assistant Professor of English "probably felt nervous when two hundred pairs of eyes stared at him" (*B.O.A.*, p. 25).

However, Malgudi has proportionally a fair number of educational institutions namely, municipal school, an old man's pyol school, the eccentric headmaster's school, Albert Mission School, St. Stephen's School, Lovedale School, Methodist Girls' School, Board High School, The Town Elementary School, Higher Elementary Town School, The Extension Elementary School, besides Albert Mission College.

So, the overcrowded schools and colleges in spite of a fairly large number of educational institutions in Malgudi reflects the increasing desire for education among Indians as observed by Gandhiji.

Significantly, the wave of education is not confined to Malgudi only. It even reaches a remote village like Mangala. Following Raju's instruction, a schoolmaster in *The Guide* opens an evening school in the pillared hall of the temple for the village children who go out to graze their cattle the whole day.

Further, the Gandhian observation with reference to the people's indifference to know the real meaning of education also seems to realize itself in Narayan's novels. Gandhiji argues that education "helps us in the building of sound character".[10] Ironically, in Narayan's novels even the characters with good educational qualification, i.e. Ramani and Shanta Bai in *The Dark Room*, Rosie in *The Guide*, Vasu in *The Man-Eater of Malgudi*, Mali and Grace in *The Vendor of Sweets*, Raman and Daisy in *The Painter of Signs* and Dr. Rann in *Talkative Man* indulge in debauchery.

Next, education became a means of serving the British in India. Gandhiji alleges that it aimed to qualify the Indians "for certain types of government jobs".[11] And it is perhaps due to the job-centred aim of education in mind, Raju's father in *The Guide* prefers to send Raju to the pyol school of an old master whose students are "now big officials at Madras, collectors and men like that" (*T.G.*, p. 26). But it nullifies the very meaning of education as Raju feels: "My father, who wanted to save me from the language of the railway trackmen, had certainly not made a safer choice in sending me to this old man, who habitually addressed his pupils as donkeys and traced their genealogies on either side with thoroughness" (*T.G.*, p. 26).

Women's emancipation draws Gandhiji's attention the most. *Women and Social Injustice* (1942) and *Women* (1958), both by M.K. Gandhi deal largely with the cause of women. Further, *Gandhi on Women* (1988) by Pushpa Joshi presents Gandhi as a liberator of women. Commenting on Gandhi's contribution to the cause of women, Hansa Mehta argues, "From the dumb, timid and suppressed creature that she was, Gandhiji made the Indian woman into a person, self-respecting, self-confident, and more assertive of her rights and at the same time conscious of her duties."[12] Gandhiji seeks to liberate women from the evils of child-marriage, dowry system and their exploitation. He firmly believes that education alone can liberate women from such evils. To quote Gandhiji:

> I have pointed out from time to time that there is no justification for men to deprive women of, or to deny to them, equal rights on the ground of their illiteracy. But education is essential for enabling women to assert these natural rights, to exercise them wisely, and to work for their expansion; again, the true knowledge of self is unattainable by the millions who lack such education.[13]

The Dark Room seems to espouse the Gandhian cause of women's education in a large measure. Reflecting on Savitri's occasional sulking, though appreciating her for the pains she takes to keep him happy and the home running, Ramani feels that "women must be educated; it made all the difference" (*D.R.*, pp. 88-89). Ramani further adds that "with a little education Savitri might have been even better" (*D.R.*, p. 89). He views education as imparting maturity to a person. Though Ramani's remark regarding Savitri is not correct, it certainly has a point, independent of the context in the novel. Savitri herself regrets: "If I had gone to a college and studied, I might have become a teacher or something" (*D.R.*, p. 120). She views education as imparting security to a person. Therefore, Savitri desires that her daughters, Sumati and Kamala "must study up to the B.A. and not depend for their salvation on marriage" (*D.R.*, p. 120).

Ironically, the Gandhian cause of women's education is espoused in *The Dark Room* by Ramani, an oppressor of Savitri, Ramani's wife, and a seducer of Mrs. Shanta Bai, a probationer in Ramani's office. However, the advocacy of women's education by Ramani, who by and large appears to be a misogynist, substantiates the impact of the Gandhian cause of women's education in *The Dark Room* at a deeper level.

Further, the Gandhian cause of women's education also echoes itself in *The Guide*. Raju's mother initially shows an aversion to Rosie due to Rosie's caste. Moreover, she is also amazed to see that Rosie has arrived unescorted. Though, Rosie's marital status and her immoral relations with Raju are not yet revealed to Raju's mother. But her aversion and strangeness about Rosie dispel on learning that Rosie is an M.A. In her appreciation of Rosie's education, Raju's mother says:

> Good, good, brave girl. Then you lack nothing in the world. You are not like us uneducated women. You will get on anywhere. You can ask for your railway ticket, call a policeman if somebody worries you, and keep your money. (*T.G.*, p. 142)

Moreover, it is interesting to note that the old female characters namely, Sriram's grandmother, Raju's mother and Raman's aunt respectively, in *Waiting for the Mahatma*, *The Guide* and *The Painter of Signs* are all illiterate. However, Raman's aunt is "literate enough to read familiar sacred texts", but doesn't know how to write "except putting her signature on the monthly receipt from the savings bank" (*P.O.S.*, p. 156). On the contrary, the young female characters are literate. Even some hold a university degree. This awareness in women's education within a short span of time of a generation implies the influence of Gandhian advocacy for a woman's education.

Though Gandhiji believes in the salvation of women through education, he teaches women to adore their household work and not to come out in public to earn. To quote Gandhiji:

> In my opinion it is degrading both for man and woman that woman should be called upon or induced to forsake the hearth and shoulder the rifle for the protection of that hearth. It is a reversion to barbarity and the beginning of the end. In trying to ride the horse that man rides, she brings herself and him down.[14]

A number of women in Narayan's novels devote themselves to their household duties. Savitri in *The Dark Room* is found worried about the health of Babu, her son. Thereafter, she advises Kamala, her younger daughter, not to come home running from her school, panting for breath in recess hour. She encourages Kamala to take her food properly. She also expresses her concern over the poor physical growth of Sumati, her elder daughter. As a devoted wife Savitri takes adequate care of the likes and dislikes of her husband. Besides, whenever she goes out she instructs the cook to look after her children properly.

Ramani's villainy and Savitri's victimization in *The Dark Room* seems to depend on the fact that Savitri does not work to earn and devotes herself to her family and the household work. Her role as a woman is underestimated by her husband.

Though, *Waiting for the Mahatma* does not refer directly to Bharati's education, Bharati is trained to "teach people spinning and tell them about Mahatmaji's ideas" (*W.F.M.*, p. 59). She is liberated but she knows her limits also. She could walk about unescorted even in the dark. Despite her love and promise to marry Sriram she would seldom surrender herself to the latter's passions. She would only wait for Gandhi's sanction to their marriage. Her devotion to duty is further seen when even as a bachelor she nurses the refugee children like a surrogate parent in a camp. She is truly what Sriram calls her "the daughter of India" (*W.F.M.*, p. 59). *The Guide* also presents Rosie conscious of her role as a woman. Even as a successful dancer and a huge wealth earned from her dance-shows, Rosie declines Raju's offer to engage a cook, saying: "I must not lose touch with my womanly duties" (*T.G.*, pp. 184-85). However, in *The Painter of Signs*, Daisy's excessive zeal for family planning, inspired by her education, certainly makes her a devoted worker, but at the expense of her lover and husband, who has rightful demands on her. And in *The World of Nagaraj* Saroja, Tim's wife, who is an M.A. shows her independent nature the way she reveals her aversion to the kitchen, passion for harmonium much to the annoyance of her father-in-law and also the way she leaves the house for Kismet, a local bar, with Tim, quite unmindful of the family's reputation to sing there for fifty rupees per night. It underlines the evil influence of English education.

Thus, Narayan's novels present Gandhi's view of woman's liberation in terms of a range of responses, from most conservative like Savitri to the most radical like Daisy, Bharati being the most ideal. Besides, they also look for and create an alternative Indian feminism to Western feminism while negotiating woman's freedom with native and traditional value system.

In view of the third component of the Gandhian education, English education as an imperialist strategy, it is essential to trace first the influence of English education in India in historical context. Vide the Resolution of Lord William Bentinck, dated 7 March 1835, English education received official recognition in India. The Resolution directed to impart "the Native population knowledge of English literature and science through the medium of the English language".[15]

With the implementation of English education, the number of English-medium schools and colleges in India began to increase in rapid succession. Apart from a large number of English-medium schools, about half a dozen English-medium colleges run by Christian missionaries were also opened at the initial stage. These include—St. Xavier's and Wilson Colleges in Bombay, Scottish Church College in Calcutta, Madras Christian College and St. Stephen's in Delhi. Besides, a few English-medium government colleges, the Presidency Colleges in Calcutta and Madras and Elphinstone in Bombay were also opened. Even the University of Bombay, the University of Calcutta and Aligarh Muslim University also implemented English as a medium of instruction. However, the University of Madras followed both English and Tamil as languages of instruction. Moreover, the teaching of English language and English literature was compulsory in these institutions. Further, the teaching of Western culture and religion in the institutions run by Christian missionaries in sheer negligence of Indian culture and religion posed a big threat. Consequently, the English education in India proved inimical to native languages, literatures, culture and religion. Mulk Raj Anand laments the damage caused by English education:

> So the scholars who were busy with Indian classical studies in the seminaries of our country, the artisans who were busy creating the subtle crafts for which the Indies had been famous, the alchemists and the practitioners of the indigenous systems of medicine, all had to shut up shop. And the heritage bequeathed to our forefathers in Sanskrit, Arabic, Persian and the mediaeval regional languages became a closed book. The religious and philosophical systems which were our great accomplishments were rendered obsolete, and the poetry which was integral to our temperament was baulked by English rhythms. The greatest tragedy was that our whole main tradition was broken. And for a hundred and fifty years we were to remain neither orientals nor Westerners, ghosts wandering about in a no man's land, reaching out now to the dim past and then to the foreign landscapes of Vilayats beyond the seas. And the vacuum was of course filled with a montage of English imagery combined to the rhythm of the Indian mind, a hotch-potch of which

> the hall-mark was bad taste. From the poetry of Kalidasa we descended to the ribaldry of the Limerick or badly written spun verse.[16]

Thus, English education proved entirely inauthentic to the Indian sensibility.

Ironically, despite the immense damage caused by English education, most of the Indians were keen to pursue it. Even some resolved to provide their children entirely a European upbringing. For example, Dr. Krishnadhan Ghosh, Sri Aurobindo's father, developed an English atmosphere for his children even at home. Later, he managed to admit his three children, including Sri Aurobindo, to the Loretto Convent School at Darjeeling, a school meant only for European children. Finally, Krishnadhan sent his children to England. There he put them under the care of Mr. Drewett, Mrs. Drewett and Dr. Walker, the eminent British scholars, under strict instructions that his sons might not be allowed to mix up with any Indian or undergo any Indian influence. Consequently, Sri Aurobindo and his brothers were left ignorant of their mother-tongue.

Caricaturing a snobbish product of English education, Lajpat Rai comments:

> He took his dress, he took his cheroot and pipe, and also his cup and beefsteak. He began to live in houses built and furnished in the English way. He detested Indian life and took pride in being Anglicised. Everything Indian was odious in his eyes. The Indians were barbarians; their religion was a bundle of superstitions; they were dirty people; their customs and manners were uncivilised; they were a set of narrow-minded bigots who did not know that man was born free. So the English set the fashion for them in everything. If their English masters went to church and read the Bible, they did the same. If the English masters indulged in free-thinking, they did the same. They wanted to be like their English masters in every way.[17]

Further, Gandhiji also sadly observes the damage caused by English education to native culture and languages:

> The foreign medium has caused brain-fag, put an undue strain upon the nerves of our children, made them crammers and imitators, unfitted them for original work and thought, and disabled them for filtrating their learning to the family or the masses. The foreign medium has made our children practically foreigners in their own land. It is the greatest tragedy of the existing system. The foreign medium has prevented the growth of our vernaculars.[18]

Though Gandhiji describes the evils of English education, he bears a great love for English language and literature. Gandhiji himself declares:

> I must not be understood to decry English or its noble literature. The columns of Harijan are sufficient evidence of my love of English.[19]

Besides, most of the speeches and writings of Gandhi are in English. The flourishing Indian writing in English has also proved the flexibility and rich complexity of English which could suit well even an Indian soil. R.K. Narayan, an Indian writer writing in English, expresses his gratitude to English: "All that I am able to confirm, after nearly thirty years of writing, is that" the English language "has served my purpose admirably, of conveying unambiguously the thoughts and acts of a set of personalities, who flourish in a small town named Malgudi (supposed to be) located in a corner of South India".[20] Besides, Narayan's love for English literature is evidenced ironically from his decision not to register himself for the M.A. in English, fearing that he would lose his interest in English literature.

Significantly, Gandhiji loves both English language and literature. Yet he still condemns English education. Similarly, Narayan appreciates English language and literature. Yet his novels interpret Gandhian ideals of education. This keeps alive the historical debate, highlighting the charms of English education.

R.K. Narayan's novels seem to record a notable spread of English education. Malgudi claims to have at least four English-medium schools, i.e. Albert Mission School, St. Stephen's School, Lovedale School and Methodist Girls' School. Though Albert Mission School is also referred to as Albert Mission High School in *The World of Nagaraj*. Besides, there is Albert Mission College too. However, the Albert Mission College is also referred to as the Christian College in *The Bachelor of Arts* and as Albert Mission Junior College in *The World of Nagaraj*. Such a large number of English-medium institutions in Malgudi, a small town, itself substantiates the preponderance of English education in Narayan's fictional world.

Moreover, the enormity of English education is traced in a Gandhian way. Almost all of Narayan's protagonists are either students or the products of English education. But true to the historical complexity, Narayan has also made English education a debatable issue in his fiction. For example, in *Swami and Friends* Swaminathan, having been punished by the Head Master of Albert Mission School, scornfully leaves it to join the Board High School with vernacular as medium. But once later the very sight of Albert Mission School fills him with love and nostalgia. In his deep appreciation for the old school Swaminathan calls it "the august Albert Mission School" (*S.A.F.*, p. 146). On the other hand, the Head Master of the Board High School is contemptuous of English education. He views Albert Mission School as "pariah school" (*S.A.F.*, p. 135). Analyzing *The Bachelor of Arts* in terms of the damage caused by English education, H.H. Anniah Gowda comments: "No doubt there was much intellectual waste as a result of British education."[21]

Further, in *The Financial Expert* Margayya, himself the Secretary of the Town Elementary School, reflects that when he accumulates huge wealth, Balu, his son, "would study, not in a Corporation School, but in the convent" (*F.E.*, p. 29). But in *The Guide* Raju's father is hostile to English education. He admits Raju far away to a pyol school "while the fashionable Albert Mission School was quite close by" (*T.G.*, p. 25). On the contrary, Raju himself shows a predilection for Albert Mission School: "I'd have felt proud to call myself an Albert Mission boy" (*T.G.*, p. 25). Again, in *A Tiger for Malgudi* the Captain's view with respect to English education contrasts with that of his wife: "You demanded that the boys should be sent to Lovedale School; that I have done, swallowing my own ideas at such a cost!" (*A.T.M.*, p. 37).

Evidently, the Gandhian dislike for English education is shared by the Head Master of the Board High School in *Swami and Friends*, Raju's father in *The Guide* and the Captain in *A Tiger for Malgudi.* But the hypnotic charm of English education is exemplified through Swaminathan in *Swami and Friends*, Margayya in *The Financial Expert*, Raju in *The Guide* and Captain's wife in *A Tiger for Malgudi* registering a common public perception, becoming stronger in modern India. Hence, Narayan's fiction accommodates the debate on English education, with its complexity.

Moreover, Gandhiji also points out the ridiculous classroom situation, which results from an inadequate and incongruent method of teaching English to a native learner. Gandhiji quotes the experience of his school days:

> But the schoolmaster's business was to drive English into the pupil's head. Therefore more than half of our time was given to learning English and mastering its arbitrary spelling and pronunciation. It was a painful discovery to have to learn a language that was not pronounced as it was written. It was a strange experience to have to learn the spelling by heart.[22]

Thus, Gandhiji also shows his concern over the unusual stress for absurd reasons on the teaching of English.

The English Teacher reflects ironically on the teaching of English in terms of Principal Brown's display of ludicrously unusual concern over a mis-spelt word. Krishnan observes:

> We were summoned to his room at the end of the day. Under normal conditions, he would welcome us with a smile, crack a joke or two, talk of nothing in particular for a couple of minutes and then state the

> actual business. But to-day we found him dry and sullen. He motioned us to our seats and said, "Could you imagine a worse shock for me? I came across a student of the English Honours, who did not know till this day that 'honours' had to be spelt with a 'u'?" He finished his sentence with a sharp, grim laugh. (*E.T.*, pp. 5-6)

Thus, the manner of teaching English embodies a colonial attitude in *The English Teacher*.

Significantly, *The English Teacher* was originally published under the title 'Grateful to Life and Death' by Michigan State College Press. Its reprint under the title *The English Teacher* brings the theme of English education into focus.

The World of Nagaraj also traces satirically the stress on the teaching and learning of English. As Nagaraj recollects his school days:

> At the Albert Mission they always punished me for my spelling, particularly words like "commit" or "receive". To this day I am never certain "receive" should be "ieve" or "eive"; it does not matter at this stage, but in those days they made me write down the word one hundred times and bring it to the class, otherwise they would make me stand outside the classroom and do it. Awful days! I wonder how I survived it at all. (*W.O.N.*, p. 129)

At home Nagaraj's father is equally particular about correctness of spelling: "Whenever I had to write an imposition, my father pulled out the red-covered dictionary and noted down in bold letters on a piece of paper "receipt", "knowledge" or whatever it was, so that I might not blunder again" (*W.O.N.*, p. 129).

Next, Gandhiji also remarks about the absurdity of imposing English on the native people:

> It did not matter to the teacher if a boy spoke bad English which he could neither pronounce correctly nor understand fully. Why should the teacher worry? His own English was by no means without blemish. It

> could not be otherwise. English was as much a foreign language to him as to his pupils. The result was chaos.[23]

The Bachelor of Arts seems to validate this Gandhian observation through Mr. Gajapathi, the Assistant Professor of English, who reads "Shakespeare in a sing-song fashion, and with a vernacular twang" and also earns "the hatred of the students by his teaching and of his colleagues by his conceit" (*B.O.A.*, p. 24).

Narayan's novels record this historical fact. In *The Bachelor of Arts*, Mohan, a poet-student of Albert Mission College writes his poems not in Tamil, his mother-tongue, but in English. And Mohan justifies his cause, saying that English "is the language of the world" (*B.O.A.*, p. 48). *The Bachelor of Arts* further refers to too "many English-speaking sanyasis" who offer "to tell the future" (*B.O.A.*, p. 113). Moreover, Chandran surveys that out of the total population of Malgudi "the English-knowing persons were at least 10,000" (*B.O.A.*, p. 127). Even the letters between Chandran and Susila, Chandran's wife, are exchanged in English.

But English as a language of human and natural sciences would not reach all sections of society. New learning, available only in English and not in vernacular would be denied to a great number of people. It would also discourage the growth of vernacular in the long run. The fictional Gandhi in *Waiting for the Mahatma* explains this colonial aspect of English to his audience:

> I will not address you in English. It's the language of our rulers. It has enslaved us. (*W.F.M.*, p. 27)

Dr. Pal in *The Financial Expert* regrets that the books on sociology are mostly written in English and not in the native languages:

> It's a subject that has been much neglected in our country—particularly in our own vernaculars, in our mother-tongue. They've everything in English, but in our mother-tongue—no. What should the thousands of people who know only our language do to learn the subject? (*F.E.*, p. 66)

But in *The World of Nagaraj*, Nagaraj proposes to write his book on Narada in English. In doing so, Nagaraj acknowledges English as an international language, proper to disseminate the cultural heritage of India. As Nagaraj himself feels: "Must write in English, of course, so that the book is widely read and people understand the concept of Narada" (*W.O.N.*, p. 44). Besides, Nagaraj argues that he "loved the English language" (*W.O.N.*, p. 97). And this love for English leads him to fancy Sanskrit, the scriptural language of India, as "a dead language" (*W.O.N.*, p. 96). This is also true to a large extent. Further, commenting on the evil caused by English education to Sanskrit, the pundit, a Sanskrit scholar, satirically remarks: "For Sanskrit studies our schools are unsuited; they are all right for English and other mlecha bashas..." (*W.O.N.*, p. 97). The text itself explains 'mlecha basha' as 'outcast's language'. This brings in the issue of tradition and modernity in the novelistic discourse.

Interestingly, the Captain in *A Tiger for Malgudi* seems to resolve the linguistic conflict in an amicable way. The Captain conveys his message in Hindi, English and Tamil, explaining:

> ...in Hindi since it is our national language and given to us by Mahatma Gandhi himself; also in English because as our beloved respected leader Nehru put it, it opens a window on the world. In Tamil, because it is, ah, our Mother-Tongue, in which our greatest poets like Kamban and Valluvar composed; also the sublime inspiring patriotic songs of Bharathi, who can ever forget them? (*A.T.M.*, p. 66)

Like English language, English literature also fascinates Narayan's characters. In *The Bachelor of Arts* Chandran finds "a real pleasure to read literature in the evenings" (*B.O.A.*, p. 18). In *The Dark Room* Gangu engages a tutor, who makes her "go through Scott's novels" (*D.R.*, p. 18). And Krishnan in *The English Teacher* echoes the Gandhian love of English literature. Krishnan reads "for the fiftieth time Milton, Carlyle and Shakespeare" (*E.T.*, p. 5). Even while saying goodbye to the teaching of English literature Krishnan reflects: "What fool could be insensible to Shakespeare's sonnets or the Ode to the West Wind or 'A thing of beauty is a joy for ever'?" (*E.T.*,

p. 178). Moreover, Krishnan tells Principal Brown that though he reveres English poets and dramatists, yet he would like to teach them to the students "in a different measure and in a different manner" (*E.T.*, p. 180). Considering the love for English literature as revealed in *The Bachelor of Arts*, *The Dark Room* and *The English Teacher*, Valentine Cunningham aptly observes:

> Most obviously, Narayan's India is trying to come to terms with English. The burden of European literature is knowingly born.[24]

Besides, *The Bachelor of Arts* laughs at the rigid pedagogic way of teaching English literature in terms of Mohan's grudge against Principal Brown:

> Go and read before the Literary Association, for the two-hundredth time, a rehash of his lecture notes on Wordsworth or Eighteenth-century Prose, and he will permit it. He won't stand anything else. (*B.O.A.*, p. 48)

Valentine Cunningham further ridicules English education from the point of view of the students and Indian professors of Albert Mission College who are "delighting adverts against the hubris of cultural imperialism".[25] Similarly, Krishnan in *The English Teacher* laughs at the rigid pedagogic way of teaching which has reduced English literature to "the dead mutton of literary analysis and theories and histories" (*E.T.*, p. 178).

Besides, Narayan's novels also display the onslaught of English literature on vernacular literatures. Mohan in *The Bachelor of Arts* by way of writing his poems in English and not in Tamil, his mother-tongue, and Nagaraj in *The World of Nagaraj* by proposing to write a book on Narada in English, and not in any of the Indian languages, essentially echo the literary onslaught. However, in *Grandmother's Tale* a night school for slum children claims to have produced some eminent "pundits in Tamil language and literature" (*G.T.*, p. 2).

Thus, *The Bachelor of Arts* and *The English Teacher* show the cultural damage caused by English education. In *The*

English Teacher the curse of English education is explained from Krishnan's point of view. Krishnan believes that the rigid pedagogic way of teaching English literature in India has reduced Indians to morons. The very imposition of Western literature in total disregard of native literatures has forced Indians to feed on "leavings and garbage" (*E.T.*, p. 178).

But the religious onslaught caused by English education is the worst. All the English-medium schools and also the Albert Mission College in Malgudi are run by Christian Missionaries. Historically, the sole purpose of the Christian Missionaries to impart education to Indians sought to proselytize them. Rev. B.W. Tucker's letter to Gandhiji lends a support to the Gandhian objections to proselytizing through education. The extract from the letter is as follows:

> I am in full agreement with you in your protest against the methods employed by Christian missions in their efforts to gain proselytes through education, medical services and the like. Education when used for such purposes is really no education at all, but merely the perpetuation of the present substitute for education initiated by the Government, which no honest missionary, familiar with educational experimentation in the lands from which he comes would tolerate for a minute if his primary interest was education rather than proselytising.[26]

Though an "honest missionary" would not use education for religious conversion, its practice did exist, as evidenced by Rev. B.W. Tucker.

Swami and Friends presents derogatory remarks about Hindu religion through Mr. Ebenezar, a Christian teacher in Albert Mission School with English as medium:

> 'Oh, wretched idiots!' the teacher said, clenching his fists, 'Why do you worship dirty, lifeless, wooden idols and stone images? Can they talk? No. Can they see? No. Can they bless you? No. Can they take you to Heaven? No. Why? Because they have no life. What did your gods do when Mohammed of Gazni smashed them to pieces, trod upon them, and constructed out

> of them steps for his lavatory? If those idols and images had life, why did they not parry Mohammed's onslaughts?' (*S.A.F.*, p. 5)

Then Mr. Ebenezar showcases the virtues of Christianity:

> Now see our Lord Jesus. He could cure the sick, relieve the poor, and take us to Heaven. He was a real God. Trust him and he will take you to Heaven; the kingdom of Heaven is within us. (*S.A.F.*, p. 5)

Prejudiced against Hinduism, Mr. Ebenezar further adds:

> Did our Jesus go gadding about with dancing girls like your Krishna? Did our Jesus go about stealing butter like that archscoundrel Krishna? Did our Jesus practise dark tricks on those around him? (*S.A.F.*, pp. 5-6)

Thus, *Swami and Friends* illustrates the way imperialism operates through an implied attempt at religious conversion.

However, the missionary's evil practice to proselytize through education also echoes in *The Guide*. Raju's father does not send Raju to Albert Mission School fearing that "they try to convert our boys into Christians and are all the time insulting our gods" (*T.G.*, p. 25). But proselytizing through education comes true in *The Painter of Signs* with reference to Daisy. After running away from her parent's house, Daisy "finally studied with the help of a missionary organization, refused baptism but changed her name to some non-denominational label, adopting the name Daisy" (*P.O.S.*, p. 155). And the protest against proselytizing is evidenced through Daisy's refusal to baptism.

Thus, the evils of English education, in linguistic, literary, cultural and religious spheres, as pointed out by Gandhiji, echo in R.K. Narayan's novels also.

In view of the fourth component of the Gandhian education, the British examination system, it is useful to mention that like English education, the British examination system also warranted Gandhi's condemnation. Under the British education system, a student had to compulsorily appear at and get through the annual examination in order to seek promotion to the next class. Vinoba Bhave, an eminent nationalist and social reformer, blames the examination system explaining that "when I used to appear for examinations there were supervisors to watch us and I used to think that if they entertained such suspicions about us, where was the wisdom in examining us, since we had already failed in their eyes".[27] However, Gandhiji condemns the examination system due to its undue strain on the nerves of students and also for making the entire process of learning and teaching as examination-centred. To quote Gandhiji: "The labour spent on studies is considered useless drudgery which has to be gone through for the sake of the final examination, and once this is over what was learnt is forgotten as quickly as possible."[28]

Swami and Friends exemplifies this undue strain on the nerves of students caused by an imminent examination:

> At school everybody seemed to be overwhelmed by the thought of the examinations. It was weeks since anybody had seen a smile on Sankar's face. Somu had become brisk and business-like. The Pea took time to grasp jokes, and seldom gave out any. And as for Rajam, he came to the school at the stroke of the first bell, took down everything the teacher said, and left at the stroke of the last bell, hardly uttering a dozen words to anybody. Mani was beginning to look worried and took every opportunity to take Sankar aside and have his doubts (that arose from time to time as he plodded through his texts) cleared. (*S.A.F.*, p. 52)

Even Swaminathan's father is so careworn that he doesn't allow Swaminathan to go out till the examinations are over.

Further, *The Bachelor of Arts* shows how the approach of examination rings the changes in learning and teaching in a college:

> In March Chandran lost about six pounds in weight. He hardly thought of anything, saw anybody, or did anything, except study. The college now existed only for the classroom, and the classroom only for the lectures. Everybody in the college was very serious and

> purposeful. Even Gajapathi now devoted less of his time to attacks on critics than to lectures that would be useful in the examination. (*B.O.A.*, p. 50)

Moreover, Margayya in *The Financial Expert* feels that Balu must take special food during examination at his school to stand the strain. Balu's examination causes Margayya a great agony. And Balu himself views examination as the "most unnecessary torment" (*F.E.*, p. 135). Further, Jagan in *The Vendor of Sweets* becomes sincere to his studies during college examinations and studies far into the night.

Next, the examination-centred learning and teaching of English education, as alleged by Gandhiji also echoes in Narayan's novels. In *Swami and Friends* Swaminathan skips "things that may not be necessary for the examination" (*S.A.F.*, p. 53). Besides, Swaminathan does not want to study for the sake of knowledge: "I mean, father, when the school is closed, when there is no examination, even then should I read?" (*S.A.F.*, p. 83). However, *The English Teacher* sneers at the examination-centred mode of education as Krishnan explains to Principal Brown:

> Sir, what I am doing in the college hardly seems to me work. I mug up and repeat and they mug up and repeat in examinations. (*E.T.*, p. 179)

Further, the examination system even forces one to use unfair ways in order to get through the examination. In *Swami and Friends* Mani, a student of First Form, who is known to have never passed his examination, eventually tries to leak out the examination papers with the help of his school clerk. Similarly, in *The Financial Expert*, grieved over his son's failure at the examinations, Margayya tends to use his influence to see his son get through the examinations next year.

Besides, a student's failure in the examination disrupts the peace of his entire family. In *The Financial Expert* Balu's failure at the matriculation examination infuriates Margayya beyond measure. Margayya's wrath shudders his wife, while Balu, always a meek and submissive boy, suddenly retaliates. Shocked by Balu's unusual behaviour, Margayya concludes that failing the matriculation has "conferred a new status on his son, and unloosened his tongue" (*F.E.*, p. 139). Further, Margayya's insistence on Balu to pass matriculation in his next trial, despite Balu's aversion to study and examinations, leads Balu to run away from his house. And later when the false news of Balu's death reaches, Margayya curses the very system of examination:

> "Did I treat him too harshly over the examination results? Or have I been too thoughtless over that cursed school-record?" He felt angry at the thought of examinations: they were a curse on the youth of the nation, the very greatest menace that the British had brought with them to India. (*F.E.*, p. 156)

Thus, the Gandhian charges against the British examination system reflect in R.K. Narayan's novels.

In view of the fifth component, national education, it is significant to point out that Gandhi's national scheme of education seeks to provide an alternative for the existing system of education. The national education scheme aims to impart education through crafts, thereby reducing the strain caused by mere bookish knowledge. Moreover, it also aims to make education self-supporting, besides discouraging the colonial aim of English education to produce clerks to run the state machinery.

Gandhiji firmly believes that a student will know more through a practical exposure to crafts than through the conventional teaching, confined to the walls of a classroom. Gandhiji describes the merits of education through crafts as under:

> Our education has got to be revolutionized. The brain must be educated through the hand. If I were a poet, I could write poetry on the possibilities of the five fingers. Why should you think that the mind is everything and the hands and feet nothing? Those who do not train their hands, who go through the ordinary rut of education, lack 'music' in their life. All their faculties are not trained. Mere book knowledge does not interest the child so as to hold his attention

> fully. The brain gets weary of mere words, and the child's mind begins to wander.[29]

Hence, Gandhiji maintains that a student will learn mathematics through spinning. To know the number of yards spun by him on the takli (an instrument to spin with), he will learn figures. A little later he will learn addition, subtraction, multiplication and division. In dealing with the complicated sums he is required to use symbols. This will teach him algebra. Besides, spinning will also teach him geometry. For, the disc of the takli itself will serve the best example of a circle.

In a similar way, spinning will also teach the child geography and history. For example, while teaching spinning to the child, the teacher is required to begin with the history of cotton—how and when cotton was first grown, the stages of its development, the cotton trade between the different countries and so on. The mention of different countries will naturally tell the child something about the history and geography of these countries. This will further enable the child to know the different commercial treaties signed during different periods. Further, the takli will lead the child to acquaint himself with the whole history of the East India Company.

The English Teacher seems to espouse the Gandhian ideal of national education and the Gandhian advocacy of education through crafts in an interesting way. The headmaster enables his school children to produce a variety of objects—cardboard houses, paper flowers and bead work, instead of educating them through these crafts. Moreover, they also draw pictures of tigers, lions and trees. The headmaster begins a child's education by teaching it a craft, echoing the Gandhian advocacy. Gandhiji observes:

> Literacy in itself is no education. I would therefore begin the child's education by teaching it a useful handicraft and enabling it to produce from the moment it begins its training.[30]

Leela makes a paper boat the very first day she is admitted to the headmaster's school. Besides, the headmaster also follows the Gandhian method of teaching a handicraft. Gandhiji observes, "Only every handicraft has to be taught not merely mechanically as is done today but scientifically, i.e. the child should know the why and the wherefore of every process."[31] The headmaster himself tells Krishnan that Leela finished her paper boat "within an hour" (*E.T.*, p. 134). It accentuates the implication that the headmaster also allows his children an ample opportunity to apply their brains to learn the intricacies of the craft.

But the sole objective of the Gandhian education through craft is to make learning quicker, spontaneous and easier. As Gandhiji puts:

> There is thus no end to the educative possibilities of this new scheme. And how much quicker the child will learn all that, without putting an unnecessary tax on his mind and memory.[32]

And in *The English Teacher* the Gandhian objective is realized by the headmaster through the game-way method. The headmaster tells Krishnan:

> Just as they play—I gather them together and talk to them and take them in and show them writing on boards. They learn more that way. (*E.T.*, p. 125)

Another objective of the advocacy of education through craft is to make every school self-supporting. To quote Gandhiji: "Thus every school can be made self-supporting, the condition being that the State takes over the manufactures of these schools."[33] But the headmaster in *The English Teacher* instead of using the crafts as a source of income, preserves them in school as "the trophies" (*E.T.*, p. 134). Nor does the headmaster's school need to sell crafts to make it self-supporting, for the headmaster maintains the utmost economy:

> This will do for a school. We are a poor country, and we can do without luxuries. Why do we want anything more than a shed and a few mats and open air? This is not a cold country for all the heavy furniture and elaborate buildings. (*E.T.*, p. 135)

Krishnan's exposure to the headmaster's system of education, based on game-way method and crafts highly impresses him. At first, Krishnan doubts the headmaster's method, thinking, "If they are always playing when do they study?" (*E.T.*, p. 125). But the headmaster's explanation and Krishnan's direct contacts with the headmaster's way of imparting education, catches Krishnan's fancy:

> I was sure there were many things about him which would fascinate me. I was seized with a desire to know more of him. (*E.T.*, p. 125)

Further, Krishnan is also impressed by the headmaster's insistence on the teaching of crafts. And this is evidenced from Krishnan's response to his daughter's product, a green paper boat: "My little Leela in relation to an outside world, making her own mark on it" (*E.T.*, p. 134).

So, Krishnan's exposure to the headmaster's method of education enables Krishnan to understand a true meaning of education. Himself a lecturer in English at Albert Mission College, Krishnan is eventually led to defy English education characteristically in a Gandhian way: "I am up against the system, the whole method and approach of a system of education which makes us morons, cultural morons, but efficient clerks for all your business and administrative offices" (*E.T.*, p. 179). It further leads Krishnan to resign his college to work as a teacher in the headmaster's school even for the one-fourth of his college salary. It substantiates the Gandhian influence of national education on Krishnan. Rama Jha supports this view: "At the end of the novel the English Teacher ceases to be an English teacher and achieves freedom to experiment with education on Gandhian lines."[34]

Thus, *The English Teacher* portrays the evils of English education in linguistic, literary, cultural and religious contexts. It interprets the Gandhian advocacy of national education through the headmaster's school, based on creative learning and teaching.

NOTES

1. Swami Nirvedananda, *Swami Vivekananda on India and Her Problems* (Calcutta: Advaita Ashram, 1995), p. 44.
2. M.K. Gandhi, "Criticism Answered", *Harijan*, V, No. 25 (July 31, 1937), pp. 196-98.

3. M.K. Gandhi, *Hind Swaraj or Indian Home Rule* (1938; rpt. Ahmedabad: Navajivan Publishing House, 2000), p. 78.
4. D.S. Sarma, "The Father of the Nation" in *Problems in Asian Civilizations: Gandhi Maker of Modern India?* ed. Martin Deming Lewis (Massachusetts: D.C. Heath and Company, 1965), pp. 9-15.
5. Chittaranjan Das, "Bengal and the Bengalees" in *Chittaranjan Das: A Biography of His Vision and Ideas*, ed. Verinder Grover (New Delhi: Deep & Deep Publications, 1998), pp. 170-209.
6. M.K. Gandhi, *The Problem of Education* (Ahmedabad: Navajivan Publishing House, 1962), p. 3.
7. N. Ranganath, "Realism in Literature: A Critique on R.K. Narayan's The Guide", *Triveni*, 48, No. 3 (Oct.-Dec. 1979), pp. 81-85.
8. Donald Barr, "A Man Called Vasu", Review of *The Man-Eater of Malgudi* by R.K. Narayan, *New York Times*, 12 Feb. 1961, p. 5, cols. 1-2; p. 16, col. 4.
9. Rita Joshi, "Vintage Narayan", *The Hindustan Times*, 22 July 1990, p. 4, cols. 6-8.
10. M.K. Gandhi, *The Problem of Education*, *op. cit.*
11. *Ibid.*
12. Hansa Mehta, *Indian Woman* (Delhi: Butala & Company, 1981), p. 109.
13. Nirmal Kumar Bose, *Selections from Gandhi* (Ahmedabad: Navajivan Publishing House, 1948), p. 255.
14. M.K. Gandhi, "What is Woman's Role?", *Harijan*, VIII, No. 2 (February 24, 1940), pp. 12-14.
15. Percival Spear, *The Oxford History of Modern India (1740* - 1947) (London: Oxford University Press, 1965), p. 206.
16. Mulk Raj Anand, *On Education* (Bombay: Hind Kitabs Ltd., 1947), p. 12.
17. Lajpat Rai, *Young India: An Interpretation and A History of the Nationalist Movement from Within* (1916; rpt. Delhi: Publications Division, Ministry of Information and Broadcasting, Govt. of India, 1968), pp. 105-06.
18. M.K. Gandhi, "National Education", *Young India*, III, No. 35 (Sept. 1, 1921), pp. 276-77.
19. M.K. Gandhi, "Higher Education", *Harijan*, VI, No. 22 (July 9, 1938), pp. 176-78.
20. R.K. Narayan, "English in India: Process of Transmutation", *The Times of India*, 3 December 1964, p. 8, cols. 3-5; p. 9, col. 5.
21. H.H. Anniah Gowda, "Literary Criticism: R.K. Narayan", *The Literary Half Yearly*, VI, No. 2 (July 1965), pp. 25-39.
22. M.K. Gandhi, "Higher Education", *op. cit.*
23. *Ibid.*

24. Valentine Cunningham, "Baboo: *The Bachelor of Arts, The Dark Room* and *The English Teacher* by R.K. Narayan", *New Statesman*, 96, No. 2491 (15 Dec. 1978), pp. 829-30.
25. *Ibid.*
26. M.K. Gandhi, "Christian Missions", *Young India*, XIII, No. 22 (May 28, 1931), pp. 121-22.
27. Vinoba Bhave, "Nai Talim", *Harijan,* XIII, No. 31 (Oct. 2, 1949), pp. 261-62.
28. M.K. Gandhi, *The Problem of Education*, *op. cit.*, p. 4.
29. M.K. Gandhi, *Basic Education* (1951; rpt. Ahmedabad: Navajivan Publishing House, 1962), p. 90.
30. M.K. Gandhi, "Criticism Answered", *op. cit.*
31. *Ibid.*
32. *Ibid.*
33. *Ibid.*
34. Rama Jha, *Gandhian Thought and Indo-Anglian Novelists* (Delhi: Chanakya Publications, 1983), p. 134.

Religious Thoughts in Gandhi and Narayan

3

India has had pronounced religious traditions. Its people observe different religions, like Hinduism, Islam, Sikhism, Christianity, Jainism and Parsi. They believe in different gods, celebrate different festivals, wear different dresses, develop different food habits and have different language preferences. Despite this diversity, the entire nation embodies the one and only religion, acclaimed universally as Indian religion. In appreciation of the religious make-up of India, Swami Vivekananda observes: "In India, religious life forms the centre, the keynote of the whole music of national life."[1]

Gandhiji was born in a Hindu Vaishnava family. The Vaishnavas are essentially religious by caste. Right from his childhood Gandhiji saw his mother visit Haveli, the Vaishnava temple, everyday and also regularly observe prayers and fastings even if she had fallen ill. This left an indelible impression in the tender mind of Gandhiji. As a young boy Gandhiji also visited the Haveli quite often. But the pomp and glitter of the Haveli did not appeal to him. Moreover, the rumours of immorality practised in the Haveli also declined his interest in the Haveli. These led Gandhiji to quest for a true religion.

Just then, following the suggestion of Rambha, his nurse, Gandhiji began to read the *Ramayana* and also chanted Ramanama (the name of Lord Rama) repeatedly. But later Gandhiji's love and devotion to the *Bhagavad Gita* grew so profoundly that he could not spare a moment without thoughts of the book. Eknath Easwaran comments, "Gandhi is first and last a child of the Gita."[2] Moreover, Gandhiji also read and loved the *Bible* and the *Koran*.

At the same time Gandhiji happened to read *Shravana Pitribhakti Nataka* (a play about Shravana's devotion to his parents) and see *Harishchandra*, a play, performed by a certain drama company. Both of them transformed the life of Gandhiji. Moved by Shravana's devotion to his parents, Gandhiji found it "an example" for him "to copy".[3] Similarly, the role of Harishchandra, the protagonist in *Harishchandra*, set before him the ideals of truth and forbearance: "To follow truth and to go through all the ordeals Harishchandra went through was the one ideal it inspired in me."[4] Moreover, through the religious discourses held frequently in his house between his father and the Jain monks and also through the Muslim and Parsi friends of his father, Gandhiji learnt about their respective faiths. This developed in Gandhiji love and goodwill for other religions.

This religious sensitivity led Gandhiji to choose a saintly life for himself. Religion became his guiding principle. Even his politics bore a religious propensity. Gandhiji declares:

> I could not live for a single second without religion. Many of my friends despair of me because they say even my politics are derived from religion. And they are right. My politics and all other activities of mine are derived from my religion.[5]

Bhikhu Parekh, an eminent scholar on Gandhian studies, aptly sums up Gandhiji's response to religion:

> For Gandhi, religion was the basis of life and shaped all one's activities. It could not be compartmentalized, reserved for special occasions or days of the week, or viewed as a preparation for another world. To be religious was to live in the constant presence of the cosmic spirit and to translate that awareness in all one did. It affected the smallest as well as the most momentous activities of one's life, including how one sat, talked, ate, and conducted one's personal,

> professional, and public life, and was nothing more than their 'sum total'.[6]

Thus, religion is central to the Gandhian thought and deed.

R.K. Narayan seems to reflect the Gandhian religious view in his novels to a large extent. Like Gandhiji, Narayan's family background is also religious. R.K. Narayan was born in a Brahmin family. In India, Brahmins are the most religious people by caste. Narayan's religious upbringing is bound to leave its imprint on his writings. Moreover, in *My Days* (1975) Narayan reveals the religious dimension of his novels. Inspired by his uncle, Narayan began to read Kamban's version of the *Ramayana* so that his "writing will gain seriousness and weight".[7] Narayan spent full three years to go through 10,500 stanzas of the book. Apart from the *Ramayana*, Narayan went through other Indian epics too. The retold legends; *Gods, Demons and Others* (1965), *Ramayana* (1972) and *Mahabharata* (1978) evidence that. However, as a student of Lutheran Mission School Narayan also read the *Bible* and was fascinated by it.

P.S. Sundaram observes Narayan's novels as "religious fables".[8] Right from *Swami and Friends* to *Grandmother's Tale* there is hardly any novel that refrains from registering at least the name of one of the Indian epics. Besides, his novels frequently refer to the important episodes from Indian epics. And some of his novels are based on the stories figuring in Indian epics. For example, *The English Teacher* uses the story of Savitri and Satyavan. *The Man-Eater of Malgudi* is based on the story of Bhasmasura. And *The Painter of Signs* is based on the story of Santanu and Ganga. Moreover, *The Dark Room* echoes the *Ramayana* and *The Guide* echoes the story of Valmiki.

Waiting for the Mahatma and *The Vendor of Sweets* bear significantly on Gandhian view of religion. In *Waiting for the Mahatma* a huge gathering awaiting the arrival of the fictional Gandhi are engrossed in chanting 'Raghupathi Raghava Raja Ram, Pathitha Pavana Seetha Ram', the litany of the historical Gandhi. In his public address Gandhi calls upon his audience to chant "Ram Dhun", do "spinning on the charka" and to follow "the practice of absolute Truth and Non-violence" (*W.F.M.*, p. 28). Thereafter, Gandhi advises Sriram to spin, read *Bhagavad Gita* and utter Ram Nam continuously. Later Gandhi conveys to Bharati through his letter how he wished that she could read Tulsi Das' *Ramayana* without any assistance. He further adds: "Wherever you may be with a copy of Ramayana and Gita, and a spinning wheel, there you are rightly occupied" (*W.F.M.*, p. 138).

And in *The Vendor of Sweets* Jagan, a follower of Gandhi, always keeps with him a red-bound copy of the *Bhagavad Gita* and frequently quotes from it to illustrate his points. Besides, Jagan also acknowledges "what he owed to Mahatmaji" (*V.O.S.*, p. 20).

The religious thoughts of Gandhiji can be divided into the following components:

1. Indomitable faith in the divine
2. Belief in the supernatural
3. Truth and non-violence
4. Immorality as a menace to religion
5. Love for all life.

In view of the first component, indomitable faith in the divine, Narayan's novels seem to share an equal faith in the divine. Gandhi's books *An Autobiography or The Story of My Experiments with Truth* (1927), *Ramanama* (1949), *My God* (1962) and *Pathway to God* (1971), K.G. Saiyidain's *Significance of Gandhi as a Man and Thinker* (1970) and *Gandhi: A Very Short Introduction* (2001) by Bhikhu Parekh deal largely with Gandhi's views on religion. Gandhiji describes his faith in God:

> I am surer of His existence than of the fact that you and I are sitting in this room. Then, I can also testify that I may live without air or water but cannot live without Him. You can pluck out my eyes but that cannot kill me. But blast my belief in God and I am dead.[9]

Narayan's novels manifest this Gandhian faith in God through various ways—prayers, pilgrimages, religious discourses, references to scriptures and the characters figuring in them, preponderance of the temples of various deities, the scriptural echo in the naming of the major characters.

Chandran's mother in *The Bachelor of Arts* first prostrates before the gods and then accepts her food. She does not let a day go without worship. Even in her hours of leisure she cannot help thinking of the divine: "As she turned the beads, her lips uttered the holy name of Sri Rama, part of her mind busied itself with thoughts of her husband, home, children, and relatives, and her eyes took in the delicate beauty of coconut trees waving against a starlit sky" (*B.O.A.*, p. 12). Savitri in *The Dark Room* declares, "I have always performed my daily pooja without fail" (*D.R.*, p. 116). And in *The English Teacher* Krishnan's mother after her arrival from the village to make up the rented house for Krishnan in Malgudi tells him that in the village she used to worship every morning. Moreover, Susila, Krishnan's wife, also shows a devout faith in God. As Krishnan observes:

> An alcove at the end of the dining room served for a shrine. There on a pedestal she kept a few silver images of gods, and covered them with flowers; two small lamps were lit before them every morning. I often saw her standing there with the light in her face, her eyes closed and her lips lightly moving. (*E.T.*, p. 36)

Further, in *Mr. Sampath: The Printer of Malgudi* the old man tells Srinivas that he worships everyday.

Besides, in *The Financial Expert* Margayya hangs a small framed picture of the Goddess Saraswati in his son's study room and enjoins him ceremoniously to pray to the Goddess every morning as he wakes up. And Raju's mother in *The Guide* reads her prayer-books everyday before her lunch, sitting before the pictures of the god, in meditation. In *The Painter of Signs* Raman reflects that his aunt has never "missed a single evening's discourse at the temple" (*P.O.S.*, p. 108). And in *The World of Nagaraj* Sita, Nagaraj's wife, mutters a prayer before the gods in her puja room everyday in the morning and visits the temple in the evening.

Further, in *The Man-Eater of Malgudi* thousands of Malgudians on a certain festival sing devotional songs, pray and place their offerings to the images of Radha and Krishna in the temple of Lord Krishna. Thereafter, they set out on a religious procession, headed by Kumar, the temple elephant, quite unmindful of Vasu's threat to kill Kumar.

However, Narayan's characters are also seen praying in their hours of agony and dismay. In *Swami and Friends*, Swaminathan, finding himself in a difficult strait at dead of night on a certain day, prays to the gods to rescue him. He promises the gods to offer "two coco-nuts every Saturday to the elephant-faced Ganapathi; a vow to roll bare-bodied in dust, beg, and take the alms to the Lord of Thirupathi" (*S.A.F.*, p. 160). Swaminathan's grandmother also prays to the god for his safe return. Similarly, in *The World of Nagaraj* when Tim walks out of house with his wife and does not return, Sita, Tim's aunt, prays and promises to the god in her temple "to light a hundred wicks if he comes back safe" (*W.O.N.*, p. 154).

The prayers of Swaminathan and his grandmother get realized. Swaminathan, who had been lying nearly dead across the road in a distant highway, safely arrives home. Swaminathan's grandmother expresses her gratitude to the "Lord of the Seven Hills to whom alone she owed the safe return of the child" (*S.A.F.*, p. 170).

Further, Narayan's characters also propitiate the divine to win some special boon. In *The Financial Expert* Balu, Margayya's son, is a boon conferred upon Margayya as a fruit of his twelve-year prayers, including a pilgrimage to Thirupathi. Later in the novel, following the advice of the priest, Margayya undertakes a forty-day penance to obtain wealth from Lakshmi, the consort of Vishnu and the Goddess of Wealth. The penance proves its efficacy as it paves a way for Margayya to his prosperity through his meeting with Dr. Pal.

That Margayya's prosperity is an outcome of his worship of the goddess, is suggested in the text itself. By the completion of the penance Margayya gets reduced to poverty as he mentally says to the goddess: "You have taken my last coin" (*F.E.*, p. 74). Earlier in the novel the priest explains to Margayya the benevolence of the goddess, saying: "When she throws a glance and it falls on someone, he becomes rich, he becomes prosperous, he is treated by the world as an eminent man, his words are treated as something of importance" (*F.E.*, p. 50). This is exactly what Margayya secures after the worship of the goddess.

Moreover, Margayya's prosperity is also an outcome of his encounter with Dr. Pal, the author of a manuscript entitled as *Bed-Life or the Science of Marital Happiness.* Because Margayya, in spite of Dr. Pal's insistence, only agrees to buy the manuscript on hearing the sound of a cycle bell, interpreting it as "the voice of God" (*F.E.*, p. 90). It is through the miraculous sale of the book, finally appeared as *Domestic Harmony*, Margayya becomes rich.

The realistic explanation of Margayya's success in the world does not negate the rewards of the penance. A rich ambiguity is available to a religious-minded reader.

Similarly, in *The Vendor of Sweets* the barrenness of Jagan's wife is cured by the worship of Santana Krishna on Badri Hill. Moreover, in *The Painter of Signs* there is an old shrine of the Goddess of Plenty in a cave, where barren women pray for three days and conceive within thirty days. When the barrenness of Sita, Nagaraj's wife, in *The World of Nagaraj* is not cured despite a forty-day penance, special pujas and pilgrimages to remote temples, the novel justifies Sita's barrenness as "a curse on her family, an ancestor having killed a King Cobra..." (*W.O.N.*, p. 47).

Narayan's novels also deal with the occult tradition quite often. In *The English Teacher* Krishnan makes a psychic communion, with the help of a medium, with his dead wife. Similarly, in *Waiting for the Mahatma* Sriram's grandmother regains her life the very moment her corpse, placed on the pyre is lit. And in *The Painter of Signs* the Goddess of Plenty comes to the hermit in a dream and commands him to build a temple and install her image therein. The hermit through his mystical power addresses "the Universal Soul directly" (*P.O.S.*, p. 76).

Besides, the hermit claims, "I can argue cobras out of my way" (*P.O.S.*, p. 76). Further, in *A Tiger for Malgudi,* a sanyasi even tames a tiger through his mystical power and engages him in a philosophical discourse. And the sanyasi describes god to the tiger in his own terms as "the Creator, the Great Spirit pervading every creature, every rock and tree, and the sky and the stars; a source of power and strength" (*A.T.M.*, pp. 157-58). Commenting on the portrayal of Indian religious belief in *A Tiger for Malgudi*, C.D. Narasimhaiah rightly observes: "Narayan's unswerving Indian faith could see the possibility of a tiger practising co-existence with a saint in a cave." [10]

Besides, Narayan's characters also devote themselves to religious discourses. In *Swami and Friends* Swaminathan's grandmother narrates to Swaminathan the story of Harishchandra. In *The Financial Expert,* the priest narrates to Margayya from the *Matsya Purana* the story of Markandeya, the boy devotee of Lord Shiva, destined to die the moment he completed his sixteenth year. Further, in his forced sainthood, Raju in *The Guide* discourses on the *Bhagavad Gita* to his audience. And in *The Vendor of Sweets* Jagan, the sweet vendor, narrates to the cooks the battle of Kurukshetra, an episode from the *Bhagavad Gita* and maintains that one should read the *Bhagavad Gita* all one's life. Jagan adds further: "Mahatma Gandhi read it to us every day" (*V.O.S.*, p. 97). Further, Raman's aunt in *The Painter of Signs* visits the shrine of Ganesha every evening to listen to a pundit's narration of the epics, which continues for more than a month.

Faith in the divine also includes fear of the divine in case of rude or sinful deeds on the part of a devotee. In *Swami and Friends* Swaminathan gets annoyed and feels like abusing the gods to find that his prayer to convert pebbles into silver coins is not granted by them. But he checks himself the very next moment realizing: "He might get on without money, but it was dangerous to incur the wrath of gods; they might make him fail in his examinations, or kill father, mother, granny, or the baby" (*S.A.F.*, p. 71). And in *The Bachelor of Arts* Chandran's mother who wished that the stealer of flowers should be handed over to the police allows him to leave respectfully simply because the flower-stealer happens to be a sanyasi. Moreover, she is seized with fear thinking, "The curse of a holy man might fall on the family" (*B.O.A.*, p. 43). In *Waiting for the Mahatma* even Jagadish, an extremist, tells Sriram:

> I have no sympathy for those who don't believe in God. I don't like fellows who speak ill of God. (*W.F.M.*, p. 210)

Further, in *The World of Nagaraj* Sita, Nagaraj's wife, even considers it "a sin to misuse God's wicks..." (*W.O.N.*, p. 140).

In *The Painter of Signs* Raman's removal of the gods from his aunt's puja room to accommodate Daisy therein, viewed by Daisy as effrontery, brings god's wrath. P.S. Sundaram notes:

> But the gods have the last laugh. The room vacated for the family planner is not destined to accommodate her. She will not even enter the house as Raman's wife.[11]

Further, a true faith in God turns even a sinner like Raju in *The Guide* into a saint and a martyr.

Besides referring frequently to Indian epics and epic characters, Narayan's novels also refer to the holy places like Kasi, Amarnath, Badrinath, Benares, Haridwar and Kailas.

The novels also abound in temples of the deities like Kapaleeswarar, Srinivasa, Thirupathi, Planetary, Krishna, Ganesha, Hanuman, Ranganatha and the Goddess of Plenty. Besides, they also abound in holy persons, fake sanyasis and sorcerers. Narayan's novels describe the holy persons variously as saint, priest, sanyasi, hermit, sadhu, pundit, guru, rishi, ascetic and swamiji—the derivatives of Indian religious tradition.

Significantly, the names of Narayan's major characters have scriptural echoes. This intensifies the religious dimension of his novels. In *The Dark Room* Savitri bears the name of Satyavan's wife from the Savitri-Satyavan myth. Further, *The Financial Expert* itself mentions that Margayya, the protagonist in the novel "had been named after the enchanting god Krishna" (*F.E.*, p. 1). Sriram in *Waiting for the Mahatma* is the name by which Lord Rama is reverentially addressed in the *Ramayana*. Even Jagadish, an extremist in *Waiting for the Mahatma* bears one of the names of the God.

Similarly, in *The Man-Eater of Malgudi* the naming of the major characters, i.e. Nataraj, Vasu and Rangi is also religious. 'Nata' is one of the thousand names of Shiva. And Shiva is also called 'Nataraja', the Lord of the dance. Vasu bears the echo of Vasudev (Lord Krishna). And the name 'Rangi', as M.K. Naik notes, "is obviously derived from 'Ranganath', one of the appellations of Vishnu".[12] Further, in *The Painter of Signs* Raman's aunt Laxmi also bears the name of the goddess. The aunt herself explains to Raman the significance of her name, a kind of playful worldly exploitation of the name of a goddess:

> I was especially fortunate as I had the name of the Goddess of Wealth, Laxmi, and no one dared say, 'Go away, Laxmi,' as it might be inauspicious. It was always good to say, 'Oh, Laxmi, welcome to our house,' and I was invited ungrudgingly into any of the hundred houses in our village. (*P.O.S.*, p. 20)

It is ironical that Raman's aunt has to leave her own house towards the end of the novel.

Further, in *The World of Nagaraj* the naming of Nagaraj and Sita have scriptural echo. The novel itself explains the meaning of Nagaraj as "the thousand-hooded serpent in whose coils God Vishnu rests" (*W.O.N.*, p. 107). Even Tim whose name offends the sadhu in the novel, is really named Krishnaji. Pleased to learn it, the sadhu says to Nagaraj:

> Do you know why we name children after the gods? So that His name in some form is always on one's lips and the walls echo divine names! (*W.O.N.*, p. 10)

In view of the second component, belief in the supernatural, R.K. Narayan's novels seem to share this belief. *Harijan* (Vol. I, No. 52) highlights Gandhiji's intrinsic faith in the superstition. Gandhiji identifies the Bihar earthquake of 1934 with the sin of untouchability. To quote Gandhiji himself: "I share the belief with the whole world—civilized and uncivilized—that calamities such as the Bihar one come to mankind as chastisement for their sins."[13]

Narayan's novels present this belief in the supernatural in an interesting way. The marriages in his novels cannot take place unless the horoscopes of the prospective bride and groom get matched. In *The Bachelor of Arts* Malathi's father claims that "the marriage of couples ill-matched in the stars often leads to misfortune and even tragedy" (*B.O.A.*, p. 86). However, in *The Financial Expert* when Balu's horoscope does not match the horoscope of the daughter of a very rich planter, Margayya, Balu's father, out of selfish gains, asks Dr. Pal to find a different astrologer to rearrange "the stars of Balu to suit the circumstances" (*F.E.*, p. 187). Thus, horoscopy becomes a strong social convention, sometimes to be managed and tackled by the shrewd, tinged with Narayan's ironic humour.

Further, in *The English Teacher,* Susila's illness leads her mother to believe that Susila is haunted by an evil spirit. And she brings in a Swamiji to cure Susila through mantras, whereas, Susila's illness is diagnosed as typhoid by the doctor. Even the doctor acknowledges Swamiji's way of treatment, though his remarks bear a tinge of irony:

> "Ah, no, don't belittle these people," said the doctor. "There is a lot in him too, we don't know. When we understand it fully I am sure we doctors will be able to give more complete cures". (*E.T.*, pp. 84-85)

But, faith in the supernatural often borders on the belief in a superstition. *Mr. Sampath: The Printer of Malgudi* presents a similar example. When after his outburst in the studio of Sunrise Pictures, Ravi becomes docile and uncommunicative, his mother is led to believe that Ravi is haunted by a ghost and can only be brought back to his normal self through exorcising.

The dramatic revival of Sriram's grandmother at the crematory in *Waiting for the Mahatma* prevents her from entering Malgudi because it was believed that the whole town would get wiped out by fire or plague if she was allowed to do so.

Moreover, in *A Tiger for Malgudi* the belief of the villagers in the supernatural strikes humour. The decrease in the number of their animals day by day makes the villagers think that their animals are eaten away by a devil. So, they prepare to "perform propitiatory ceremonies in their villages" (*A.T.M.*, p. 26). Whereas, the animals are killed by the tiger.

Narayan's novels are primarily concerned with Indian way of life. As Chetan Karnani observes: "Narayan's themes are usually built round Indian beliefs and superstitions".[14]

In view of the third component, truth and non-violence, it is significant to maintain that Narayan's novels refer to the principles of truth and non-violence to a large extent. Truth is the sole objective of Gandhiji's entire life. And he observed non-violence strictly in thought, word and deed. Gandhiji's speeches and writings frequently refer to his doctrines of truth and non-violence. "The basic foundation of religion" for Gandhiji, according to K.G. Saiyidain, "rested on the twin pillars of truth and non-violence, their relative priority in that order".[15]

In addition to a printing press named as 'Truth Printing Works' in *The Bachelor of Arts*, *Mr. Sampath: The Printer of Malgudi*, *The Vendor of Sweets* and *The World of Nagaraj* and a weekly named as *The Truth* in *The Guide*, *Waiting for the Mahatma* champions the Gandhian doctrine of truth and non-violence. The character of Gandhi in *Waiting for the Mahatma* while addressing a large gathering on the sands of Sarayu in Malgudi advocates "the practice of absolute Truth and Non-violence" (*W.F.M.*, p. 28).

Further, Bharati explains to Sriram the essence of Gandhian truth, which applies to day-to-day living:

> None except absolute truth-speakers are allowed to come into Mahatma's camp. People who come here must take an oath of absolute truth before going into Mahatma's presence. (*W.F.M.*, p. 55)

She further adds that the Mahatma "will not mind anything at all, but you will have to speak the truth if you speak at all" (*W.F.M.*, p. 61).

In a similar way, Savitri in *The Dark Room* has a reverence for truth. Savitri reflects: "I've never lied in my life, except a few uttered in childhood" (*D.R.*, p. 116). And also later in *The*

Dark Room the priest of the old village temple urges Ponni, Mari's wife, to "utter the strictest truth" (*D.R.*, p. 174). Moreover, in *The Financial Expert*, despite his dubious identity and activities, Dr. Pal has a reverence for truth, who claims: "I'm an academician and I'm only interested in Truth and how human beings face it" (*F.E.*, p. 85).

Further, in *The Vendor of Sweets* Jagan, a follower of Gandhi, feels impelled to tell Grace a lie, respecting her sentiments. But understanding the value of truth, Jagan "silently prayed to Gandhi's spirit to forgive the lie he was about to utter" (*V.O.S.*, p. 64). However, Raman in *The Painter of Signs* approaches truth as a complex issue. Having returned unfed from the inauguration of the lawyer's office and having been told by the aunt that she was observing a fast, Raman refrains from speaking the truth. Raman justifies his cause, reflecting:

> On three occasions you need not speak the truth. To save a life, to save an honour...and the third I can't remember, but I suppose to save an aunt the bother of cooking for you. (*P.O.S.*, p. 15)

Here truth is defined in the context of life. It is replaced by love and compassion.

Thus, Narayan's characters reveal their deep faith in truth. Even a mean and demonic character like Vasu in *The Man-Eater of Malgudi* remains truthful to his vow, not to hit anyone unless he is hit first. Only once does Vasu hit his master when the latter calls him an ungrateful dog and other names and tries to push him out. And even when provoked by the inspector, Vasu does not hit him. Vasu takes the inspector by the shoulder, propels him to the cot and pushes him down. To demonstrate his strength to the inspector Vasu brings his palm flat down on the iron frame of the cot and cracks it.

Similarly, Raju in *The Guide*, moved by the villagers' faith in him, resolves to remain faithful to the prayers and fastings in order to bring rain. Raju's commitment to his vow wins Velan's appreciation. Velan respectfully tells Raju:

> Your penance is similar to Mahatma Gandhi's. He has left us a disciple in you to save us. (*T.G.*, p. 107)

But the Gandhian doctrine of non-violence seems to find an elaborate treatment in Narayan's novels. Even as an apostle of non-violence Gandhiji himself admits that violence is an inborn instinct in human beings. This belief expresses itself in *A Tiger for Malgudi*. The master of the tiger observes: "Every creature is born with a potential store of violence" (*A.T.M.*, p. 145). Further, Srinivas in *Mr. Sampath: The Printer of Malgudi* views violence as "the despair of Gandhi" (*M.S.P.M.*, p. 95). And Srinivas views non-violence as "one of the paths of attaining harmony in life" (*M.S.P.M.*, p. 95). To propagate the message of non-violence, Srinivas even proposes to produce and screen a film in which Ram Gopal, the hero of the film, would be "a disciple of Gandhi's philosophy, practising ahimsa (non-violence) in thought, word and deed" (*M.S.P.M.*, p. 98).

In *Waiting for the Mahatma* Gorpad, a volunteer in Gandhi's camp, realizing the virtue of non-violence argues, "Mahatma will not let me be violent even in thought" (*W.F.M.*, p. 76). Similarly, Nataraj in *The Man-Eater of Malgudi* also acknowledges the merits of non-violence: "Mahatma Gandhi had enjoined on us absolute non-violence in thought and speech, if for no better reason than to short-circuit violent speech and prevent it from propagating itself" (*M.O.M.*, p. 58). And while dealing with the violent Vasu, Nataraj tackles violence through non-violence, inviting Narayan's ironic treatment:

> Vasu might after all not be facing the window, but facing the door. Non-violence would be the safest policy with him. Mahatma Gandhi was right in asking people to carry on their fight with the weapon of non-violence; the chances of getting hurt were much less. (*M.O.M.*, p. 163)

Moreover, in *Waiting for the Mahatma* the fictional Gandhi appeals to Sriram to walk barefoot rather than "wear sandals made of the hide of slaughtered animals" (*W.F.M.*, p. 78). He advises Sriram to wear sandals made out of the skin of an animal who has met a natural death. And once when due to certain reason such a leather doesn't reach Bharati from Wardha, Bharati is seen walking barefoot, complying with Gandhi's message. Besides, Jagan in *The Vendor of Sweets* also practises the message of Gandhi. "Being a follower of Gandhi", Jagan explains, "I do not like to think that a living creature should have its throat cut for the comfort of my feet" (*V.O.S.*, p. 9). And this occasionally involves Jagan in excursions to remote villages to secure hide of the animal reported to be dying.

Further, Narayan's novels also portray the strength caused by the practice of non-violence. Gandhi's message of non-violence in East Bengal during communal violence inspires even the aggressive rowdy-looking men to take "a vow of non-violence and a vow to protect the opposite faction" (*W.F.M.*, p. 244). Similarly, in *A Tiger for Malgudi* the Captain's exposure of the tiger to the philosophy of non-violence in the Grand Malgudi Circus by allowing the tiger to sip milk in the company of a goat, and later the Master's discourse on non-violence train the tiger to show "great concern and self-control" (*A.T.M.*, p. 144). It is, therefore, Narayan declares that "*A Tiger for Malgudi* is his own favourite, perhaps the reason why Gandhi exhorted that the Rishis who practised non-violence were greater geniuses than Newton and greater warriors than Wellington."[16]

Moreover, the Gandhian movements like Satyagraha, Civil Disobedience, Non-Cooperation, Dandi March and Quit India, referred frequently to Narayan's novels, are based on the doctrine of non-violence. Violence in Narayan's novels cannot last long. In *The Man-Eater of Malgudi* the violent Vasu faces his death ironically in a non-violent way. P.S. Sundaram observes: "Violence in any form, Narayan feels, is evil, a thing to be avoided."[17]

Notably, the Gandhian doctrine of non-violence has invited various kinds of comments. People like Tilak and M.N. Roy criticized it severely. M.N. Roy viewed non-violence as "a premium on consummate hypocrisy".[18] On the contrary, people like Einstein, Martin Luther King Jr., Pearl S. Buck, Jawaharlal Nehru and Dalai Lama interpreted Gandhian non-violence as a unique weapon to combat violence. To quote Einstein:

> Revolution without the use of violence was the method by which Gandhi brought about the liberation of India. It is my belief that the problem of bringing peace to the world on a supranational basis will be solved only by employing Gandhi's method on a large scale.[19]

Jagadish in *Waiting for the Mahatma* expresses such versions of non-violence. Despite his use of khadi clothes and his earlier association with Gandhi, he takes a recourse to the acts of violence such as setting of fire to the law courts, derailing, explosion of bomb. Sriram's initiation into Gandhian philosophy and his later recourse to violent acts under the guidance of Jagadish implies the complexity of the principle of non-violence in a real, historical context.

In view of the fourth component, immorality as a menace to religion, it is to be argued that often the Western and the Indian ways of life interact, influencing many lives. The attitudes of Babu and Sumati, Ramani's son and daughter, in *The Dark Room* reflect this. Babu prefers to go to see the English films like Curly Top and Frankenstein while Sumati doesn't like English films. She would love to see Kuchela, a film based on the boyhood of Lord Krishna and his friend Kuchela. The cultural conflict is further traceable in *Mr. Sampath: The Printer of Malgudi* with Indian theme 'Burning of Kama' of Sunrise Pictures and De Mello of Hollywood as the brain behind the studio organization. However, the shooting of the film mocks at Indian religion and it also paves a way for the immoral relations between Sampath and Shanti, a widow. Commenting on the conflict between the Western and Indian values, William Walsh observes that Narayan's novels present "the special flavour of Malgudi, a blend of oriental and pre-1914 British, like an Edwardian mixture of sweet mangoes and malt vinegar".[20]

The spread of Western ways and their alluring effect on Indians posed a threat to Indian religion. Gandhiji notes:

> The tendency of the Indian civilization is to elevate the moral being, that of the Western civilization is to propagate immorality. The latter is godless, the former is based on a belief in God.[21]

The Bachelor of Arts however, contrasts the Western mode of living with that of Indian in moral terms, indicating the demerits of traditionally orthodox Indian society:

> The white fellows are born to enjoy life. Our people really don't know how to live. If a person is seen with a girl by his side, a hundred eyes stare at him and a hundred tongues comment, whereas no European ever goes out without taking a girl with him. (*B.O.A.*, p. 15)

The Dark Room registers the onslaught in terms of immorality and breach of Indian conventions. Shanta Bai, herself a lover of unconventional things with her good education and modernity, allows herself to be seduced by Ramani. Shiv K. Girla views:

> The darker shades of moral aberrations are first noticed in *The Dark Room*. Ramani, temperamentally a callous man, violates the traditional family morality under the influence of modernity symbolised by the coquettish Shanta Bai with her Greta Garbo manners.[22]

But Shanta Bai's education underlines the positive aspect of Western civilization.

Significantly, the naming 'Engladia Insurance Company' of the office where Ramani has been serving for years and Shanta Bai just recruited as a probationer, suggests a conflict in terms of the Western and Indian values. Shanta Bai's penchant for the Western way of life and its hypnotic charm on Ramani, lead him to ignore his family, especially his wife.

Similarly, in *The Guide* Rosie's educational qualification as an M.A., her deviation from family tradition as temple dancer to perform public shows, even her Western name, altogether seem to pave a way for her moral degeneration. Similarly, Raju's rejection of traditional jibba and the lace-edged dhoti for dashing bush-shirts, corduroys, hair- and face-lotions and perfumes of all kinds in order to impress Rosie, paves a way for his moral degeneration.

Further, in *The Man-Eater of Malgudi* Vasu's intrusion violates the sacred traditions of Nataraj's press. Vasu with his enormous physical strength, demonic nature, gun, jeep, educational qualification, insatiable sexual urge and profession as a taxidermist, epitomizes the threat of Western civilization. Donald Barr rightly observes: "Vasu and the print-shop might be the West and India, might be science and humanism, might be totalitarianism and liberal civilization."[23] Besides, Nataraj's practice of monogamy is also set in contrast with Vasu's association with Rangi and other women of mean character.

In the same vein, Mali, influenced by the Western ways in *The Vendor of Sweets*, takes to beef-eating, lives immoral life with Grace and later gets arrested by the police on the charge of keeping half a bottle of wine in his car. Mali's insulting remark on cow not only upsets Jagan but also marks Mali's degeneration.

To safeguard Indian religion against the onslaught of Western civilization, Gandhiji advises "every lover of India to cling to the old Indian civilization even as a child clings to the mother's breast"[24] Shanti, in *Mr. Sampath: The Printer of Malgudi*, ashamed of her sinful life with Sampath, eventually chooses a decent life for her by returning to her son. Further, Rosie in *The Guide* eventually returns to her husband. And Raju after his release from the prison resolves to undertake fasting and prayer eventually to atone for his sins, without considering any worldly gains. And in *The Vendor of Sweets* Jagan sends excerpts to Mali from the shastras and Gandhi's writings on the cow to restore Mali to the Indian religious tradition.

In view of the fifth component, love for all life, it is useful to learn that Gandhiji himself was an apostle of love. The Gandhian love has an all-embracing nature. Gandhiji himself explains:

> I want to realise brotherhood or identity not merely with the beings called human, but I want to realise identity with all life, even with such beings as crawl on

> earth. I want, if I don't give you a shock, to realise identity with even the crawling things upon earth, because we claim common descent from the same God, and that being so, all life in whatever form it appears must be essentially one.[25]

Narayan's novels seem to express this all-embracing nature of love. They also record love for animals. In *Swami and Friends* Swaminathan's love for ant is revealed the way he is anxious to save the ant's life. And when he fails to save the ant, Swaminathan utters "a prayer for the soul of the ant" (*S.A.F.*, p. 33). And Krishnan's mother in *The English Teacher* treats the cow with love and reverence. In the morning she goes near the cows only after she has cleaned the house and taken her bath. Further, *The Vendor of Sweets* presents Jagan's love for the cow the way he responds to Mali's insulting remark on cow and considers it as a sacrilege. Vasu, the villainous character in *The Man-Eater of Malgudi* is a hunter of all kinds of animals, in an excessive manner. His cruelty towards life in general also underlines his villainy. Moreover, *The Man-Eater of Malgudi* presents the love of the people of Malgudi for the temple elephant. Having learnt of Vasu's threat to shoot the elephant on a certain festival, they appeal to Vasu and even quarrel with him to spare the elephant's life.

Besides, the Swamiji, the master of the tiger in *A Tiger for Malgudi* retorts the school teacher for using the word 'brute' for the tiger. Moreover, the Swamiji enlightens people by telling them that the tiger "has only the appearance of a tiger, but he is not one—inside he is no different from you and me" (*A.T.M.*, p. 146).

Narayan's novels echo Gandhiji's love for children also. The headmaster in *The English Teacher* loves his school children very much. When he watches them he gets "a glimpse of some purpose in existence and creation" (*E.T.*, p. 125). And in *The Financial Expert*, Margayya, enraged by the mischief slaps his son fiercely, allowing himself to be viewed by the onlookers as a "ruffian" and a "heartless demon" with their deep sympathy for the son (*F.E.*, p. 42).

Waiting for the Mahatma presents vivid example of the Gandhian love for children. The fictional Gandhi distributes the garlands and fruits presented to him, among children. He is "very keen that children should be free and happy" (*W.F.M.*, p. 92). Moreover, he makes a dirty untouchable boy sit beside him on the divan and then smooths out the boy's matted hair with his fingers. And Bharati's love for children is evidenced in the refugee camp in New Delhi where she is found nursing the refugee children devotedly.

Thus, Narayan's novels share Gandhian love for animals and children.

NOTES

1. Swami Vireswarananda, *The Complete Works of Swami Vivekananda*, Vol. III (Almora: Advaita Ashrama, 1932), p. 220.
2. Eknath Easwaran, *Gandhi the Man* (Northamptonshire: Turnstone Press Ltd., 1983), p. 106.
3. M.K. Gandhi, *An Autobiography or the Story of My Experiments with Truth* (1927; rpt. Ahmedabad: Navajivan Publishing House, 2004), p. 6.
4. *Ibid.*, p. 7.
5. K.G. Saiyidain, *Significance of Gandhi as a Man and Thinker* (1970; rpt. New Delhi: Ministry of Information and Broadcasting Govt. of India, 1994), p. 25.
6. Bhikhu Parekh, *Gandhi: A Very Short Introduction* (New York: Oxford University Press Inc., 2001), pp. 44-45.
7. R.K. Narayan, *My Days* (Delhi: Orient Paperbacks, 1986), p. 101.
8. P.S. Sundaram, "Naipaul on Narayan", *The Journal of English Studies*, 17 (1977), pp. 129-37.
9. K.G. Saiyidain, *Significance of Gandhi as a Man and Thinker*, *op. cit.*, pp. 25-26.
10. C.D. Narasimhaiah, "Makers of Indian English", *The Literary Criterion*, XXXIV, No. 1 (1999), pp. 5-32.
11. P.S. Sundaram, "Naipaul on Narayan", *op. cit.*
12. M.K. Naik, *Dimensions of Indian English Literature* (New Delhi: Sterling Publishers Pvt. Ltd., 1984), p. 146.
13. M.K. Gandhi, "Bihar and Untouchability", *Harijan*, I, No. 52 (Feb. 2, 1934), p. 1.
14. Chetan Karnani, "Critique of an Author: The Paradox of R.K. Narayan", *The Times of India*, Dec. 22, 1968, p. 10, cols. 2-4.

15. K.G. Saiyidain, *Significance of Gandhi as a Man and Thinker*, *op. cit.*, pp. 30-31.
16. C.D. Narasimhaiah, "Makers of Indian English", *op. cit.*
17. P.S. Sundaram, "Naipaul on Narayan", *op. cit.*
18. M.K. Gandhi, "Is Congress a Hindu Organisation?", *Harijan*, VII, No. 41 (November 18, 1939), pp. 341-43.
19. Albert Einstein, "On Peace—and Gandhi" in *Profiles of Gandhi*, ed. Norman Cousins (Delhi: Indian Book Company, 1969), pp. 99-100.
20. William Walsh, "Nataraja & the Packet of Saffron: The Indian Novel in English", *Encounter*, XXIII, No. 4 (October, 1964), pp. 78-83.
21. M.K. Gandhi, *Hind Swaraj or Indian Home Rule* (1938; rpt. Ahmedabad: Navajivan Publishing House, 2000), p. 55.
22. Shiv K. Girla, *R.K. Narayan: His World and His Art* (Meerut: Saru Publishing House, 1984), p. 193.
23. Donald Barr, "A Man Called Vasu", Review of *The Man-Eater of Malgudi* by R.K. Narayan, *New York Times*, 12 Feb. 1961, p. 5, cols. 1-2; p. 16, col. 4.
24. M.K. Gandhi, *Hind Swaraj or Indian Home Rule*, *op. cit.*
25. M.K. Gandhi, "My Conception of Patriotism", *Young India*, XI, No. 14 (April 4, 1929), pp. 107-08.

Socio-Economic Dimension in Gandhi and Narayan

4

Tradition refers to a social, economic or a political attitude which a nation shared in the past and which is also being practised by that nation today. However, modernity with its scientific and progressive outlook stands for a fresh attitude. And the dialectics of tradition and modernity in the context of the colonized India is a quest for a possible synthesis of socio-economic strands and its applicability in a real context.

For instance, the cloth industry in India before the advent of the British in the form of the East India Company enjoyed a distinct status. In those days spinning was not a vocation restricted to a particular class. A large number of Indians, irrespective of their class, used to spin everyday. The cloth produced then served not only national needs, but a fairly good deal was also sent abroad. But the East India Company with its unfair means monopolized trade and soon established its vast empire. Consequently, khadi, the traditional cloth industry of India, declined to the extent that in 1921, on the basis of the statistical data, Gandhiji observed that far from exporting cloth, India was importing forty crore pounds of yarn worth sixty crores of rupees to meet her pressing needs.

Therefore, Gandhiji attempts to resuscitate khadi by employing the masses of India in spinning:

> If we want to save all this money we must begin spinning. Just think how many thousands of men could be provided with employment, if these sixty

> crores of rupees were invested in industries in our own country.[1]

Further, Gandhiji observes that like khadi, tanning was also a large industry in India in her olden days. But the imperialist strategy of the British lured the educated Indians away from their vocational crafts, including tanning, and enticed them into the government jobs in such a way that they began to look down on their traditional crafts. Consequently, like other crafts, tanning also declined considerably. Expressing his regret over this decline, Gandhiji argues that rupees nine crores worth of raw hide is annually exported from India and that much of it is returned to her in the shape of manufactured articles. Therefore, to restore tanning Gandhiji recommends tanning for all—both the Harijans and non-Harijans.

Similarly, mechanization, a symbol of modernity, also caused a damage to the traditional village industries in India. Gandhiji sadly notes:

> Little flour mills are ousting the chakkies, oil mills the village ghani, rice mills the village dhenki, sugar mills the village gur-pans, etc. This displacement of village labour is impoverishing the villagers and enriching the monied men.[2]

Thus, Gandhiji condemns machinery primarily on two grounds. It displaces the village industries. It renders the villagers jobless. As a result, the poor are becoming more poor and the rich more rich. Besides, he also condemns the railway on the pretext that the railway enables the crafty and licentious people to spread evil rapidly from one place to the other.

Therefore, Gandhiji appeals to every Indian to shun machinery and to promote village industries for the economic and moral liberation of India.

Further, the villagers, tempted by the luxuries and ample job opportunities, began to migrate to the cities. Consequently, the simple and innocent village-life was set in an ironic contrast with a crafty and mechanical life of the city as a result of urbanization. So, Gandhiji appeals to the people of India to prevent urbanization and to go back and recreate neat, clean, hygienic and self-sufficient villages.

Moreover, caste discrimination and untouchability, the age-old evil of Indian society, has deplorably undergone a change. In the Vedic age a man's class was determined by his character and occupation, and not by his parentage, as it is done today. For example, in those days if a Brahman was engaged in any occupation other than his own, he was directly admitted into the class which followed that occupation. And if a Shudra was found to be a man of noble character following a learned profession, he was viewed as a Brahman. The *Vayupuran* contains a long list of Kshatriyas like Vishvamitra who became Brahmans on account of their austerities. Lord Indra, the son of Brahma (Brahman), became a Kshatriya as he took up a military career. Further, a Shudra became a Brahman if he acquired proficiency in the Vedas. And in a similar way, a Brahman became a Shudra, if he gave up the study of the Vedas.

Caste discrimination and untouchability in ancient times had a rationale. But later it fossilized in a dead, irrational convention. It has become a sin against humanity in the present times. So Gandhiji warrants its immediate abolition through purification:

> We all become untouchables every day when we attend to natural functions, and our untouchability is cured by simple ablutions. Indeed, even wicked thoughts make us untouchable, but we are cured by resisting them and purifying ourselves by taking the name of God as Ram or Vasudev or Narayan or Shiva and invoking His never-failing protection. Even so is a Harijan, whose occupation may render him untouchable, cured by prescribed purification.[3]

Untouchability does not reside permanently in a few people. And in a sense, we all are untouchables for some time. The components of the Gandhian socio-economic thoughts are as follows:

1. Rural orientation, khadi and tanning

2. Mechanization
3. The village-city encounter
4. Caste discrimination and untouchability.

In view of the first component it is worthwhile to learn that Gandhiji recommends khadi for the masses of India primarily on economic ground. Gandhiji's *The Problem of Education* (1962) mentions that about 85 per cent of India's population are engaged in agriculture, 10 per cent in crafts and the rest of the 5 per cent belong to the class of employed people. Gandhiji regrets that even as the largest industry, agriculture fails to cater to the requirement of one-tenth of India's population. Sometimes a farmer fails to cover even the cost of seed. Moreover, agriculture does not occupy the entire time of a villager. Therefore, khadi may emerge as a subsidiary industry to supplement agriculture.

Both in his speeches and writings Gandhiji lays a considerable stress on khadi. His *Economics of Khadi* (1941) advocates the use of khadi. Besides, "The Birth of Khadi", thirty-nineth chapter (Part V), "Found at Last!", 40th chapter (Part V), "An Instructive Dialogue", 41st chapter (Part V) of his autobiography, and his "The Music of the Spinning Wheel", 29th chapter of *India of My Dreams* (1947) also deal extensively with khadi. Further, the articles—"The Uses of Khaddar" (*Young India* Vol. II, No. 17), "For Lovers of Khaddar" (*Young India* Vol. II, No. 19), "Abusing the Khaddar" (*Young India* Vol. III, No. 6), "Handloom vs. Spinning Wheel" (*Young India* Vol. VIII, No. 45), "Khadi—A New Orientation" (*Harijan* Vol. II, No. 32), "Mission of Khadi" (*Harijan* Vol. III, No. 21), "Is Khadi Economically Sound?" (*Harijan* Vol. IV, No. 19), "The Charkha" (*Harijan* Vol. VII, No. 49), "Swaraj through Spinning" (*Harijan* Vol. X, No. 13) and "Khadi Science School in Bombay" (*Harijan* Vol. X, No. 16) reveal Gandhiji's concern with khadi.

Though Gandhiji had not seen a handloom or spinning wheel even by the time he returned from South Africa in 1915, he describes a spinning wheel as the panacea for the growing pauperism of India in *Hind Swaraj*, written in 1908. Only when the Sabarmati Ashram was founded, Gandhiji introduced a few handlooms there. The members of the ashram resolved to use hand-woven cloth made from Indian yarn only. This enabled Gandhiji to know from direct experience the economics and mission of khadi. For him khadi is an embodiment of the economic, cultural and political liberation of India.

Spinning is an easy means of earning bread for those who have no other work possible or available to do. Next, spinning wheel can be placed in the hands of millions of people without snatching work away from a single man. Thus, khadi can grow as an honest industry, promote self-reliance and hope. Moreover, spinning may work as a deterrent against indiscriminate use of machinery, and the modern mad rush for material comfort and Western ways. Thus, Gandhiji views khadi as "the symbol of unity of Indian humanity, of its economic freedom and equality".[4]

R.K. Narayan's novels, particularly *Waiting for the Mahatma* and *The Vendor of Sweets* largely advocate the use of khadi. The fictional Gandhi in *Waiting for the Mahatma* regards khadi as a key to India's freedom. And it is explained from Sriram's point of view: "Khadi alone was going to save the nation from ruin and get the English out of India, as that venerable saint Mahatmaji explained untiringly" (*W.F.M.*, p. 33). Similarly, Jagan in *The Vendor of Sweets* argues, "Gandhi had prescribed spinning for the economic ills of the country" (*V.O.S.*, p. 121). Moreover, *Talkative Man* mentions that anyone clad in khadi begets respect and he is treated as "a nationalist, a follower of Mahatma Gandhi" (*T.M.*, p. 73).

Further, the Gandhian postulate of khadi insists that each villager should spin regularly and produce khadi for his own use. To quote Gandhiji:

> Just as the villagers cook their own roti or rice so must they make their own khadi for personal use. The surplus if any they may sell.[5]

Khadi is understood to be as important as food, so much fundamental to human life. *Waiting for the Mahatma* echoes this Gandhian call. The fictional Gandhi urges Sriram to "take a vow to wear only cloth made out of your own hands each day" (*W.F.M.*, p. 67). And following this, when Sriram spins yarn enough for his cloth, he secures in exchange, woven cloth of the same count from a central depot at Madras. A little later the fictional Gandhi directs Bharati and Sriram to surrender themselves to the nearest police station. But he also asks them to make sure that they spin their quota even in jail.

Similarly, *The Vendor of Sweets* also refers to Gandhiji's call to spinning. Jagan spins every day for an hour. His jibba and dhoti are both made of material spun with his own hands. He also delivers the excess material in neat bundles to the local handloom committee in exchange for cash. Even towards the close of the novel when Jagan retires to the forest to live a secluded life there, he carries with him his spinning wheel, recollecting:

> It's a duty I owe Mahatma Gandhi. I made a vow before him that I would spin every day of my life. I've got to do it, whether I'm at home or in a forest. (*V.O.S.*, p. 176)

Gandhiji sublimates spinning and identifies it with his every day worship:

> Therefore, I have described my spinning as a penance or sacrament. And, since I believe that where there is pure and active love for the poor there is God also, I see God in every thread that I draw on the spinning wheel.[6]

This sacramental status of spinning appears in *Waiting for the Mahatma*. The character of Gandhi tells Sriram that "spinning a certain length is my most important work: even my prayer comes only after that" (*W.F.M.*, p. 67). Besides, he urges the people of Malgudi to follow "Ram Dhun; spinning on the charka and the practice of absolute Truth and Non-violence" (*W.F.M.*, p. 28). Moreover, during the course of his visit to the famine-affected villages, the character of Gandhi, among many other things speaks to the villagers about spinning and religion. He also advises Sriram to spin and read *Bhagavad Gita*, and utter Ram Nam continuously. Moreover, he explains to Bharati and Sriram: "Wherever you may be with a copy of Ramayana and Gita, and a spinning wheel, there you are rightly occupied" (*W.F.M.*, p. 138). Thus, the character of Gandhi in *Waiting for the Mahatma*, like the historical Gandhi, accords a sacred status to spinning.

Further, spinning soothes Jagan's mind in *The Vendor of Sweets* in a similar way as meditation does. The slight whirring noise of the wheel and touch of the thread to Jagan appear "very comforting, stilling the nerves and thoughts" (*V.O.S.*, p. 121). Moreover, spinning also relieves Jagan from a deep agitation of the mind.

Many characters appear, dressed in khadi, in Narayan's novels. In *Swami and Friends* an earnest-looking man, addressing the citizens of Malgudi on the right bank of Sarayu on 15th of August 1930, is clad in khadi. Besides, the novel also portrays a couple of boys wearing khadi caps. And in *Mr. Sampath: The Printer of Malgudi* Srinivas's late landlord's son-in-law who comes to Srinivas to claim rent, is also seen wearing a khaddar jibba.

Further, in *Waiting for the Mahatma* Bharati appears in a white khaddar sari the very day the fictional Gandhi addresses the public gathering in Malgudi. Besides, other volunteers, attending to the fictional Gandhi are also clad in khadi. Mr. Natesh, the Municipal Chairman, his wife and their son are also seen clad in khadi. Mr. Natesh even substitutes khaddar hangings in his luxurious house for gaudy chintz. Jagan in *The Vendor of Sweets* wears a loose jibba over his dhoti. In *The Man-Eater of Malgudi* the chairman of the municipal council always wears a white Gandhi cap as an unwavering member of the Congress Party. Moreover, in *The World of Nagaraj*, the servant of Dr. Velu at Velu Medical Hall is seen in a khaddar jibba and a white Gandhi cap.

But wearing khadi does not always ensure faith in Gandhian values. Gandhiji is aware of the misuse of khaddar. He is grieved to learn that many people are using "the khaddar dress as a cloak for their deceit".[7] Natesh, the Municipal Chairman, and Jagadish exemplify it in *Waiting for the Mahatma*. B.A. Pathan comments: "The municipal chairman in *Waiting for the Mahatma* is one such opportunist, who uses khaddar and Gandhiji's name for selfish ends."[8] And Renate

Sarma also describes Jagadish as a "tempter" in the "disguise of khadi".[9]

Gandhi's khadi scheme was recommended and popularized by a majority of Indian nationalists. Dr. Rajendra Prasad, the first President of India, proposed the use of khadi by all, except for the military personnel and the police. Vinoba Bhave sponsored khadi scheme. Jawaharlal Nehru also praised khadi scheme. Moreover, Kakasaheb Kalelkar prophesied that "an Indian going abroad will not hesitate to put the charkha and the hand-loom before the most industrialized people of the world".[10] This faith in khadi is exemplified by the character of Gandhi and Bharati in *Waiting for the Mahatma* and Jagan in *The Vendor of Sweets*. The character of Gandhi encourages everyone to spin and wear khadi. Bharati retains her spinning wheel even when she stays in a camp with refugee children in New Delhi.

Interestingly, *Waiting for the Mahatma* reveals Sriram's expedient attitude to khadi. In fact, it is not due to his faith in khadi, but owing to his spell for Bharati, Sriram initiates into khadi. Sriram's very glance at Bharati, wearing a khaddar sari, transforms Sriram's attitude to khadi—from a fad into a lovely thing. And later Sriram's indulgence in terrorist activities under the influence of Jagadish who is also wearing a khadi dress, confirms Sriram's lack of faith in khadi.

Moreover, it is notable that Ghanashyamdas Birla, a leading industrialist, objected to khadi in economic context stating that it yielded miserably very low wages "Not more than four annas a day and even that was very doubtful."[11] But khadi also means spiritual values. Though Jagan's wages are low in *The Vendor of Sweets*, i.e. less than five rupees a month, he is thrilled while receiving his wages for khadi.

In view of tanning, Gandhiji believes that tanning in India is as ancient as India itself. "No Need for a Tannery" (*Harijan* Vol. I, No. 39) describes tanning as an honourable and lucrative profession. It also recommends tanning for all—the Harijans and non-Harijans. And "Village Tanning and Its Possibilities" (*Harijan* Vol. II, No. 30) deals with tanning at length. Like khadi Gandhiji also lays a considerable stress on tanning. But in view of non-violence he suggests that a tanner should deal "only with the carcass, not the slaughtered animal".[12] In fact, a few tanneries in the country such as one at Sabarmati Ashram and the other at Wardha worked on Gandhian lines.

The character of Gandhi and Bharati in *Waiting for the Mahatma* and Jagan in *The Vendor of Sweets* advocate tanning with non-violence. The character of Gandhi tells Sriram that he "should prefer to go barefoot rather than wear the hide of an animal killed for your sake, that is if you are unable to secure the skin of an animal that has died a natural death" (*W.F.M.*, p. 78). He further adds that the Wardha tannery specializes in manufacturing footwears out of the hide of dead animals. And Bharati would prefer to walk uphill barefoot rather than using a leather other than one received from Wardha: "I have not yet got the leather from Wardha, and I shall have to manage with this until we get it" (*W.F.M.*, p. 99). Moreover, Jagan seems to follow Gandhi's dictates of tanning:

> He draped his shoulders in a khaddar shawl with gaudy yellow patterns on it and shod his feet with thick sandals made out of the leather of an animal which had died of old age. Being a follower of Gandhi, he explained, "I do not like to think that a living creature should have its throat cut for the comfort of my feet," and this occasionally involved him in excursions to remote villages where a cow or calf was reported to be dying. (*V.O.S.*, p. 9)

Thus, Jagan secures the hide.

After having secured the hide Jagan goes through tanning in the back veranda of his house with the help of his six-year old son. Finally, Jagan gives this hide to an old cobbler in Malgudi who manufactures Jagan's footwear out of it. It is Jagan's non-violent footwear following Gandhiji's idea.

In view of mechanization, it is notable that *Hind Swaraj* presents a sheer condemnation of machinery. Gandhiji blames machinery for having impoverished India. He even argues that machinery, the chief symbol of modern civilization, represents a great sin. However, some of the prominent nationalists like

Nehru criticized Gandhiji for his alleged attempt to take India back to the bullock cart age. Nehru's letter of October 9, 1945 to Mahatma Gandhi disagrees with Gandhi's objection to machinery, stating that modern means of transport as well as many other modern developments must continue and be developed. Nehru stresses that there "is no way out of it except to have them".[13] Gandhiji modifies his objection to machinery later, saying that what he objects is not machinery but the indiscriminate use of it:

> Dead machinery must not be pitted against the millions of living machines represented by the villagers scattered in the seven hundred thousand villages of India. Machinery to be well used has to help and ease human effort. The present use of machinery tends more and more to concentrate wealth in the hands of a few in total disregard of millions of men and women whose bread is snatched by it out of their mouths.[14]

Thus, displacement of labour and unequal distribution of wealth are equated with the harmful machinery.

The Nehru-Gandhi debate on machinery is echoed in *The Vendor of Sweets* in terms of Mali's unbridled passion for the story writing machine, juxtaposed by Jagan, who is "bewildered by his son's scheme and distrusted it totally" (*V.O.S.*, p. 86). Mali fancies that the story writing machine is going to cut time and distance and lift the country out of its rut. Moreover, he swaggers:

> I have learnt valuable things in the United States at a cost of several thousand dollars. Why can't our country make use of my knowledge? (*V.O.S.*, p. 125)

Jagan is equally amazed to see Grace's interest in Mali's story writing machine.

Thus, Jagan distrusts the story writing machine. But he also longs to see his manuscript come out of Nataraj's press which is also a machine. This echoes Gandhiji's earlier and modified statements regarding machinery. And the story writing machine with its imaginary make-up and the fuss it creates all over Malgudi, Mali and Grace being the most crazy about it, reflects Gandhiji's objections to machinery.

The destructive potential of machinery is first felt with the attempt of Mali and Grace to persuade Jagan to invest in their story writing machine and Jagan's aversion to it. Jagan could notice "the shock on Mali's face and the embarrassment he had created before Grace" (*V.O.S.*, p. 89). But Mali and Grace do not leave Jagan there. They continue to pester him. Mali, who never used to seek Jagan earlier, begins to intrude even into Jagan's puja room. And Grace studies Jagan's movements and times her interception perfectly. Jagan tries to evade them. He would tiptoe to the kitchen from his puja room. And from the kitchen he would further slip away with the least noise. In case Jagan is in the house and hears Mali and Grace opening the front door, he would retreat far into the backyard or lock himself in the bathing shack.

This kind of hide and seek creates a silent tension in the family at the initial stage which aggravates in due course of time. Mali adopts a bullying tone, Grace shows her indifference to Jagan.

Mali is not only crazy about the story writing machine, he is also contemptuous of his father's lucrative business of sweetmeats. Mali cannot accept Jagan's offer to take up the shop and run it himself. And Jagan cannot part with money for the story writing machine. Consequently, the family disintegrates. Mali gets arrested on the charge of keeping half a bottle of wine in his car. Jagan goes to the forest in retreat. While Grace flies back to the United States.

Thus, *The Vendor of Sweets* portrays the evil wrought by machinery in terms of disintegration of a family.

Moreover, *The Vendor of Sweets* also presents the evils of machinery in terms of immorality. It is the story writing machine which alone tempts Grace to come to India and live a sinful life while posing to live and behave like an Indian married woman. She would call Jagan father. She would observe fasts, wash the doorsteps, decorate the threshold with white flour and make floral designs on the ground in the manner of a traditional Hindu woman. But she does it only to impress Jagan and extract money from him. As Jagan feels:

> Had she shown all that considerateness only in order that he might invest in their story machine? Now that he had made his position clear, the barrier between him and the other two was growing more impregnable than ever, and there was absolutely no way of his approaching her and asking for an explanation. (*V.O.S.*, p. 128)

Thus, for Grace machinery is more important than any social conventions.

Further, Grace's craze for machinery at the cost of her moral degeneration substantiates itself from the very fact that she reveals her sinful life only when there is no hope for the story writing machine. Mali also explains Grace's intention to Jagan: "She came here to work, and she is going back because she has no work to do" (*V.O.S.*, p. 127). And Mali's interest in Grace vanishes as the prospect of the machine frustrates. Grace herself tells about Mali: "Mo has no more use for me" (*V.O.S.*, p. 134). Mali does not hesitate to send Grace back to America after having seduced and squandered her two thousand dollars. Thus, for Mali machinery is more important than Grace's chastity and career.

And the immorality of Mali and Grace shocks Jagan. He feels that they have "tainted his ancient home" (*V.O.S.*, p. 135). To avoid the sin further he insulates himself in his house from the evil company of Mali and Grace and retires to the forest eventually in his quest for peace.

Interestingly, Jagan blames Mali and Grace for tainting his ancient home, though he has a knowledge of the immorality practised by his grandfather's brother who "was certainly married to three wives and had numerous other women" (*V.O.S.*, p. 137). Jagan's ironic comment strikes humour.

The World of Nagaraj records the spread of mechanization far into the villages. These villages are supplied with pesticides, chemical fertilizers, machinery, the gas plant and even mechanical gadgets for threshing, slicing and mashing cattle feeds. Besides, the government gives a subsidy, cement and technical staff, in order to "modernise rural life" (*W.O.N.*, p. 54).

Further, *Swami and Friends*, *Waiting for the Mahatma* and *The World of Nagaraj* also follow the Gandhian call to popularize hand-spun cloth and boycott the mill-made cloth. Gandhiji emphatically declares that it is "due to Manchester that Indian handicraft has all but disappeared".[15] In *Swami and Friends* two young School going boys, Swaminathan and Mani resolve to "boycott English goods, especially Lancashire and Manchester cloth" (*S.A.F.*, p. 94). A couple of boys wearing Gandhi caps also move around and beg people to burn their foreign cloth. Besides, the novel also describes the crowd engaged in making a bonfire of mill-made clothes.

Similarly, Sriram in *Waiting for the Mahatma* burns mill-manufactured clothes the very moment he receives khadi clothes:

> On the day he got his Khadi clothes, a simple dhoti and a jibba (cut and stitched on the spot by the village tailor), he took off the clothes he had been wearing (mill manufactured), heaped them in the middle of the street, poured half a bottle of kerosene over the lot, and applied a match; his old clothes caught fire and burned brightly. (*W.F.M.*, p. 99)

Instantly, Sriram resolves not to wear the mill manufactured clothes in future.

And *The World of Nagaraj* describes Gopu, engaged in picketing foreign goods through the recollections of Nagaraj: "Also I remembered he used to picket liquor shops and stores selling foreign cloth by lying across the doorway in those days when young men joined the satyagraha movement started by Mahatma Gandhi" (*W.O.N.*, p. 168).

In the context of the village-city encounter, it should be noted that village, the smallest unit, forms the nucleus of social life in Gandhiji's ideal of swaraj (home rule). Gandhiji loves the village dearly. But he is against urbanization. "Penetrating the Villages", eighteenth chapter (Part V) of Gandhiji's autobiography, "Back to the Villages", his *Village Swaraj* (1962), eighth chapter of Shakuntala Masani's *The Story of Bapu* (1952) and *Gandhiji and Village* (1981) by Sheo Kumar Lal, illustrate well the Gandhian predilection for the village and prejudice against the city.

Gandhiji considers village as the soul of India. He even predicts that "if the village perishes India will perish too".[16] Narayan's novels seem to present the Gandhian faith in the village in a variety of ways. Though Malgudi is not a village, it is certainly a small town only, with a river and hills, when R.K. Narayan's career as a writer begins. Then like any other village in India, it has become wider and more advanced. Charles W. Mann refers to Malgudi as the "famous Indian village of Malgudi".[17] The Lawley Extension, South Extension, New Extension, Market Road, Ellaman Street, Kabir Street, Abu Lane, Nallappa's Grove, Mempi Hills and Sarayu River, form the major landmarks of Malgudi. The expansion of Malgudi like many Indian villages is quite slow. Its topography changes very slowly only. *Swami and Friends* (1935) describes Ellaman Street as the last street of Malgudi. And Ellaman Street continues to remain the last outpost of Malgudi eastward even in *A Tiger for Malgudi* (1986). However, the Market Road emerges as the life-line of Malgudi. Like any other Indian village, Malgudi is also susceptible to industrialization. *Mr. Sampath: The Printer of Malgudi* (1949) records the transformation of Malgudi from "a semi-agricultural town to a semi-industrial town" (*M.S.P.M.*, p. 26). And in *The Vendor of Sweets* (1967) Jagan's ancestral home which had been the last house outskirting Malgudi, becomes the first one for all the newer colonies. Further, *The World of Nagaraj* (1990) mentions that the New Extension has come up "not only on the market boundary but also other developments beyond the railway level crossing" (*W.O.N.*, p. 109).

But despite these changes Malgudi retains its identity. Jagan in *The Vendor of Sweets* argues, "After all, Malgudi is a small town; everyone is within shouting distance" (*V.O.S.*, p. 66). Moreover, *The Painter of Signs* portrays Malgudi as "unused to modern life" (*P.O.S.*, p. 146). Thus, Malgudi continues to behave like a village.

In addition to Malgudi, the villages provide a fictional landscape for Narayan's novels. This setting ranges from Sukkur village to Kommal. *The Dark Room* (1938) tells that Sukkur is only a couple of miles from Malgudi. While, Kommal is "the farthest village, nearly fifty kilometres from Malgudi" (*A.T.M.*, p. 66). Within this range fall a number of villages—Kuppam, Solur, Aruna, Mangala and Koppal, to name a few. Further, Margayya's clients in *The Financial Expert* are chiefly from the villages. And the fictional Gandhi in *Waiting for the Mahatma* attaches so much value to his visit to the villages, affected by the famine, that he has "set aside all his other engagements" (*W.F.M.*, p. 88). Besides, the novel also presents Sriram and Bharati, moving from village to village to propagate Gandhi's message among villagers. And in *The Guide* after Raju's release from the prison, village Mangala provides a setting for the novel. Moreover, in *The Painter of Signs* Daisy, after having finished her family planning campaign in Malgudi, shifts her attention to the nearby, and then to the distant villages. And also in the end, she leaves for the villages, far away in the forests to fulfil her mission there.

Gandhiji does not romanticize a village. He regrets the insanitary condition of villages:

> And so, instead of having graceful hamlets dotting the land, we have dung-heaps. The approach to many villages is not a refreshing experience. Often one would like to shut one's eyes and stuff one's nose; such is the surrounding dirt and offending smell.[18]

Waiting for the Mahatma describes the poverty-ridden village as "Hungry, parched men and women with skin stretched over their bones, bare earth, dry ponds, and miserable tattered thatched roofing over crumbling mud walls, streets full of pits and loose sand, unattractive dry fields" (*W.F.M.*, p. 89).

Though Gandhiji acknowledges the Indian village with poverty and backwardness, he envisions an ideal village:

> An ideal Indian village will be so constructed as to lend itself to perfect sanitation. It will have cottages with sufficient light and ventilation, built of a material obtainable within a radius of five miles of it. The cottages will have courtyards enabling householders to plant vegetables for domestic use and to house their cattle. The village lanes and streets will be free of all avoidable dust.[19]

Similarly, *Waiting for the Mahatma* presents Sriram's ideal village as one with "green coconut groves, long and numerous steps leading down to the large tank, with elegant village women coming up bearing pitchers, and the temple spire showing beyond the tank bund, low roofed houses with broad pyols, and mat-covered waggons moving about dragged by bulls with tinkling bells around their necks, the cartmen singing all the time" (*W.F.M.*, p. 87).

Further, Gandhiji bears a great faith in the basic goodness of the villager. Mr. Friedman, an engineer by profession, attacks the villagers charging them with stagnation. But Gandhiji defends the villagers in *Harijan*:

> But the moment you talk to them and they begin to speak, you will find that wisdom drops from their lips. Behind the crude exterior you will find a deep reservoir of spirituality.[20]

Narayan's novels also portray the basic goodness and so the vulnerability of the villagers. In *The Bachelor of Arts* the gullible people in a certain village, taking Chandran's make-up of a sanyasi at its face value, beg of Chandran "to stay for some days more" (*B.O.A.*, p. 110). In *Waiting for the Mahatma* Sriram, while propagating Gandhi's message from village to village, is "glad to find himself fussed over and treated with respect by the villagers" (*W.F.M.*, p. 87). Moreover, in *A Tiger for Malgudi* the Captain of the Grand Malgudi Circus visits a certain village which is haunted by the tiger. The Captain is so warmly received by the villagers that he feels "overwhelmed by their hospitality" (*A.T.M.*, p. 41).

However, the spirituality in the villagers also reflects in *The Guide* in terms of their faith in Raju's sainthood. Despite

Raju's confession of his sinful life before Velan, Velan continues to pay his obeisance to Raju. Like Velan, other villagers also revere Raju. This paves the way for Raju's spiritual salvation. Raju realizes:

> They might drag him back to the spot and punish him for fooling them. It was not even this fear; he was perhaps ready to take the risk, if there was half a chance of getting away. But he felt moved by the recollection of the big crowd of women and children touching his feet. He felt moved by the thought of their gratitude. (*T.G.*, p. 111)

Thus, the villagers play a catalytic role in transforming Raju, the sinner, into a saint. Fakrul Alam also acknowledges the role of the "villagers like Velan" who "apotheosise Raju-types".[21]

Besides, Gandhiji's love for the village is also characterized by his prejudice against the city. Gandhiji views the city as "a snare and a useless encumbrance" which breeds in "gangs of thieves and robbers, prostitution and vice".[22]

Narayan's novels also echo this objection against the city. *The Bachelor of Arts* presents the prejudice against the city in terms of Chandran's return to Malgudi from Madras. After having experienced the harsh realities of city-life in Madras, Chandran realizes, "The thought of Malgudi was very sweet" (*B.O.A.*, p. 102). Chandran finds the people in Madras "so mechanical and impersonal" (*B.O.A.*, p. 95). Besides, Gandhiji's dislike for the city and love for the village also come true in terms of Kailas' indulgence in wine and prostitution and Chandran's escape from Kailas, a villainous character. Chandran feels:

> There was no use remaining in the city any longer. It was so big and confusing that one didn't know even the way out of it. There was, moreover, the danger of being caught again by Kailas. (*B.O.A.*, p. 103)

Further, *The Vendor of Sweets* also refers to the city dwellers as "fussy" (*V.O.S.*, p. 152). And Daisy in *The Painter of Signs* despite her Western ways, pours scorn on city-life:

> Living in a city is not the real life. Urban life is standardized, and meant to keep people apart. (*P.O.S.*, pp. 57-58)

Gandhiji loves the village so dearly that he often longs to go and settle in a village. He also advises his co-workers to go and settle in villages:

> I have been asking all my co-workers who are doing village work to go and settle in villages and to serve the villagers. I feel that I cannot do so effectively until I go and settle in a village myself.[23]

Narayan's novels also echo Gandhiji's desire to settle in the village. The fictional Gandhi in *Waiting for the Mahatma* during his visit to the famine-affected villages desires to stay though temporarily, at the lowliest hut in the village if it was available. Similarly, Daisy in *The Painter of Signs* opens out her heart: "Ultimately I'll select the tiniest hamlet and live in a hut" (*P.O.S.*, p. 58).

Next, Gandhiji's love for the villages evidences itself from his speeches and writings, which lay a considerable stress on the uplift of villages. His speeches and writings repeatedly state that about 70 per cent of India's population dwell in her 7 lakh villages. Narayan's novels also seem to record the statistical data with reference to the number of villages almost with Gandhian sensibility. Bharati in *Waiting for the Mahatma* while passing through a village with Sriram in their mission to propagate the teachings of fictional Gandhi among villagers, tells Sriram: "There are seven hundred thousand other villages more or less like this in our country" (*W.F.M.*, p. 88). And Daisy in *The Painter of Signs* tells Raman that there are "a million villages in our country" (*P.O.S.*, p. 177).

It is to be noted that R.K. Narayan finds Indian reality reflected well in a small town or a village like Malgudi, but he himself would like to be a city-dweller:

> I cannot stay in a village. I like to watch villages while I am passing by in a car or train. But I would not like to live there.[24]

With his characteristic irony, humour and sophistication, he keeps the village at a distance in his fiction. Gandhiji's preference to the village over the city has been debatable. Jawaharlal Nehru criticizes Gandhiji on this ground. The extract of Nehru's letter spells it out:

> A village, normally speaking, is backward intellectually and culturally and no progress can be made from a backward environment. Narrow-minded people are much more likely to be untruthful and violent.[25]

Narayan's novels also present Nehru's viewpoint. In *The Bachelor of Arts* Chandran's uncle who lives in Madras tells Chandran that "staying in Malgudi would not lead him anywhere" (*B.O.A.*, p. 52). He further advises Chandran "to go to a big city and see people" (*B.O.A.*, p. 52). Besides, *The Bachelor of Arts* juxtaposes Gandhiji's response to a villager with that of Nehru: "They were innocent and unsophisticated, in most matters (excepting their factions and fights), and took an ascetic's make-up at its face value" (*B.O.A.*, p. 110). Thus, the violent tendency in the villagers as Nehru alleges is also referred to in *The Bachelor of Arts*.

Further, the villagers in *The Guide* become so violent that they hit one-another with crowbars, knives and axes at night. They even set the hay on fire. On hearing the shrieks of the villagers Raju would conclude:

> The village people do not know how to remain peaceful. They are becoming more and more agitated. (*T.G.*, p. 96)

The village-city encounter finds a true expression in *The World of Nagaraj*. Tim is prejudiced "against village life" and Nagaraj openly expresses his "aversion to the smell of cattle and cattleshed" (*W.O.N.*, p. 51). While Gopu, a village peasant, loves the village and "dabbles in mud and manure like a baby" (*W.O.N.*, p. 54).

Thus, Nehru's idea about village also reflects in Narayan's novels. Narayan's fiction accommodates the whole debate about the issue of the village and the city.

In view of caste discrimination and untouchability, it is useful to mention that Gandhiji's fight against this age-old evil brought a mixed response in an orthodox social milieu. It infuriated the orthodox Hindus but won the appreciation of the prominent nationalists like Rabindranath Tagore and Vinoba Bhave. The orthodox Hindu leaders accused Gandhiji of a dangerous heresy. They often organized black-flag demonstrations, heckled Gandhiji and attempted to disrupt his meetings. Further, when Gandhiji began his fast on September 20, 1932 in protest of the award of separate electorates for the untouchables, Rabindranath Tagore, dressed in black, spoke to a large gathering at Shantiniketan on the significance of Gandhiji's fast and the urgency of fighting this age-old evil of untouchability. Similarly, Vinoba Bhave at the prayer meeting on January 7, 1949 at the Gandhi Tatvajnan Institution, Dhulia suggests public scavenging for one and all on Sarvodaya Day (January 30, 1949, the first death anniversary of Gandhiji) as a tribute to Gandhiji and also to purge Indians of the sin, committed by treating the sweepers as untouchables.

"Outcaste", the XIIth chapter (Part I) of M.K. Gandhi's autobiography and the articles—"Untouchability" (*Harijan* Vol. I, No. 1), "Fast for Purification" (*Harijan* Vol. I, No. 13), "Bihar and Untouchability" (*Harijan* Vol. I, No. 52), "Cochin Untouchability" (*Harijan* Vol. V, No. 17), "Curse of Untouchability" (*Harijan* Vol. VIII, No. 16), "Shocking if True" (*Harijan* Vol. X, No. 7), "Why Bhangi Quarters?" (*Harijan* Vol. X, No. 8) and "Caste Corrosion" (*Harijan* Vol. X, No. 13) strongly advocate the abolition of caste discrimination and untouchability in India.

Waiting for the Mahatma and *The Vendor of Sweets* directly refer to the Gandhian concern over the evil of caste and untouchability. In *Waiting for the Mahatma* "Mahatmaji spoke of untouchability and caste" (*W.F.M.*, p. 30). And in *The Vendor of Sweets* Jagan in his reply to Grace's complaint against caste discrimination in India, argues, "Gandhi fought for its abolition" (*V.O.S.*, p. 66).

According to Gandhiji, untouchability as practised today is "a sin against God and man and is, therefore, like a poison slowly eating into the very vitals of Hinduism".[26] Similarly, he condemns caste discrimination:

> Soil corrosion eats up good soil. It is bad enough. Caste corrosion is worse, it eats up men and divides men from men.[27]

Narayan's novels begin to portray the evil of caste discrimination and untouchability from *The Dark Room* (1938) onwards. In *The Dark Room* Savitri, a Brahmin woman, attempts suicide on a certain night by drowning in the river. Incidently, Mari, a blacksmith and a burglar, who happens to return empty-handed from his night prowls, saves Savitri. After having rescued Savitri, he leaves her on the river fearing that he has been identified by her as a thief. But, next day in the morning, both Mari and his wife, Ponni, come to see if Savitri is all right. Finding Savitri alone and helpless on the river, they request her to go back to her husband. On Savitri's refusal to do so, they kindly bring her along to their village and offer her utmost hospitality. Smitten with the evil of caste and untouchability, Ponni hesitates to shelter Savitri:

> I will clear a part for you and never come there. I will buy a new pot for you, and rice, and you can cook your own food. I will never come that way. (*D.R.*, p. 137)

Though they are poor, they try to become as hospitable as possible to Savitri.

Thus, Savitri, an upper caste Brahmin, is precisely saved by Mari, an untouchable, and also treated kindly and sympathetically by Mari and his wife.

Further, *The Bachelor of Arts* presents the evil of caste in its worst form. One may learn through Chandran that an orthodox family like Chandran's will not allow a marriage between a boy and a girl even if they belong to the sub-sect of the same caste. And Chandran pours his contempt on caste discrimination: "If India was to attain salvation these watertight divisions must go—Community, Caste, Sects, Sub-sects, and still further divisions" (*B.O.A.*, p. 56).

The Financial Expert presents caste as a stigma. Margayya and his family, known as agriculturists and supposed to be of good caste presently, inherit their ancestral caste as corpse-bearers, simply because Margayya's father's grandfather and the grandfather's brothers maintained themselves as corpse-bearers. Though, none would bother about Margayya's caste secret, except a great aunt who would if provoked, taunt occasionally: "It's written on their faces—where can it go, even if you allow a hundred years to elapse?" (*F.E.*, p. 184).

Gandhiji believes that untouchability determined on the ground of ancestral occupation, is the worst of its kind.

Moreover, *Waiting for the Mahatma* also refers to the fate of the untouchables through a dark, shabby and ill-dressed untouchable boy, who attracted by the crowd enters Mr. Natesh's house only to incur Mr. Natesh's prejudice. Mr. Natesh is highly critical of Gandhi on the issue of untouchability and blames him for bringing in "such a dirty boy, an untouchable, up the steps and make him so important?" (*W.F.M.*, p. 48).

Besides, Sriram's grandmother, with her degenerated orthodoxy, would not let the scavenger, who comes everyday to sweep the backyard of her house, approach nearer than ten yards. She also habitually adopts a bullying tone while addressing him. And she also blames Gandhi for his attempt "to bring untouchables into the temples" (*W.F.M.*, p. 62). And the novel describes the place where the untouchables dwell awfully with garbage, offal, flesh, hide and the stench. This marginal space is outside the town limits, beyond Nallappa's Grove, where nobody goes. And the untouchables are restricted to use only a part of the river on its downward course.

There are kinds of untouchability. Sometimes it is not based on a particular low caste. It refers to a religion other than Hinduism, and a profession, considered to be disreputable. Such untouchables are punished with ostracization. In *The Guide* on Rosie's arrival, Raju's mother shows her aversion, wondering "how she was going to accommodate a 'Rosie' in her home"

(*T.G.*, p. 140). Raju's maternal uncle commands Rosie to get out, saying:

> After all, you are a dancing-girl. We do not admit them in our families. (*T.G.*, p. 169)

Further, Jagan's sister in *The Vendor of Sweets* rebukes Jagan for sheltering Grace:

> We are ashamed to refer to you as a brother. Even when you joined Gandhi and lost all sense of caste, dining and rubbing shoulders with untouchables, going to jail and getting up to all kinds of shameful things, we didn't mind. But now is it a fact that you have a beef-eating Christian girl for a daughter-in-law? I can hardly call you a brother in the presence of my in-laws. (*V.O.S.*, pp. 141-42)

And Jagan's elder brother, an orthodox man, who manages the headquarters of a religious order, is so upset with Jagan on this issue that he never invites him to attend the anniversary ceremonies of their father. Similarly, Raman's aunt in *The Painter of Signs* protests against Raman's marriage with Daisy, considering Daisy to be a Christian.

But Sriram in *Waiting for the Mahatma* justifies Gandhi's fight against untouchability. Bharati and the fictional Gandhi prefer to name the refugee children after the names of flowers and birds only to avoid the abuse of caste and religious discrimination. The fictional Gandhi believes that "even a number would be better than a name, if a name meant branding a man as of this religion or that" (*W.F.M.*, p. 245). Further, Raju in *The Guide* shelters Rosie in his house and protests against his orthodox mother and maternal uncle. Moreover, Raju views Rosie's caste (the temple dancers considered as public women) as "the noblest caste on earth" (*T.G.*, p. 84). And Mali in *The Vendor of Sweets* stays with Grace in his house and thus condemns the evil practice of caste and untouchability. Moreover, Raman in *The Painter of Signs* appeals to his aunt to let him marry Daisy, explaining that Daisy is also "a human being just like you or me" (*P.O.S.*, p. 147).

Remarkably, untouchability is practised by the characters who belong to old generation, namely, the great aunt, Mr. Natesh, Sriram's grandmother, Raju's mother and maternal uncle, Jagan's sister and elder brother and Raman's aunt. Only Jagan is an exception. While the younger generation like Sriram, Raju, Mali and Raman mark their disbelief in untouchability. It shows a considerable decline in the evil of caste and untouchability and reflects the debate of orthodoxy and modernity. Sriram in *Waiting for the Mahatma* who earlier derives a devilish pleasure from his grandmother's ill-treatment with the scavenger, gets transformed on listening to Gandhi's lecture on caste and untouchability. Sriram reflects: "There must be a great deal in what he says" (*W.F.M.*, p. 30). Further, Jagan, himself a follower of Gandhi, encourages Gandhi's mission to eradicate untouchability. But Raju, Mali and Raman with their penchant for Western ways, essentially underline the influence of Western civilization, uncorrupted by decayed Indian orthodoxy. Gandhian critique precisely bears on this degenerated orthodox belief in Indian society.

NOTES

1. M.K. Gandhi, *The Problem of Education* (Ahmedabad: Navajivan Publishing House, 1962), p. 25.
2. M.K. Gandhi, "Is Khadi Economically Sound?", *Harijan*, IV, No. 19 (June 20, 1936), p. 145.
3. M.K. Gandhi, "My Supposed Inconsistency", *Harijan*, II, No. 39 (November 9, 1934), p. 308.
4. M.K. Gandhi, *Constructive Programme: Its Meaning and Place* (1941; rpt. Ahmedabad: Navajivan Publishing House, 2003), p. 10.
5. M.K. Gandhi, "Mission of Khadi", *Harijan*, III, No. 21 (July 6, 1935), p. 164.
6. M.K. Gandhi, "My Kamadhenu", *Young India*, VIII, No. 20 (May 20, 1926), p. 187.
7. M.K. Gandhi, "Abusing the Khaddar", *Young India*, III, No. 6 (February 9, 1921), p. 41.
8. B.A. Pathan, *Gandhian Myth in English Literature in India* (New Delhi: Deep & Deep Publications, 1987), p. 89.
9. Renate Sarma, "Initiation and Quest—R.K. Narayan's *Waiting for the Mahatma*", *The Aligarh Journal of English Studies*, 20, No. 2 (1998), pp. 124-40.

10. K.G. Mashruwala, "The Sarvodaya Conference—II", *Harijan*, XIII, No. 4 (March 27, 1949), pp. 28-29.
11. Vinoba Bhave, "A Challenge to Sarvodaya Philosophy", *Harijan*, XIV, No. 15 (June 10, 1950), pp. 129-30.
12. M.K. Gandhi, "Village Tanning and Its Possibilities", *Harijan*, II, No. 30 (September 7, 1934), pp. 236-37.
13. Jawaharlal Nehru, *A Bunch of Old Letters* (1958; rpt. Bombay: Asia Publishing House, 1960), pp. 507-11.
14. M.K. Gandhi, "Fallacies", *Harijan*, III, No. 31 (September 14, 1935), p. 244.
15. M.K. Gandhi, *Hind Swaraj or Indian Home Rule* (1938; rpt. Ahmedabad: Navajivan Publishing House, 2000), p. 81.
16. Mahadev Desai, "Prevention of Exploitation—Passive and Active", *Harijan*, IV, No. 29 (August 29, 1936), p. 226.
17. Charles W. Mann, "Narayan, R.K. Gods, Demons and Others", *Library Journal*, 89, No. 19 (November 1, 1964), p. 4359.
18. M.K. Gandhi, *Constructive Programme: Its Meaning and Place*, *op. cit.*, pp. 13-14.
19. M.K. Gandhi, "A Humble Villager of Birbhum", *Harijan*, IV, No. 48 (January 9, 1937), p. 383.
20. Pyarelal, "Limits of Industrialization", *Harijan*, VI, No. 51 (January 28, 1939), pp. 438-39.
21. Fakrul Alam, "Narrative Strategies in Two Narayan Novels" in *R.K. Narayan: Critical Perspectives*, ed. A.L. McLeod (New Delhi: Sterling Publishers Pvt. Ltd., 1994), pp. 8-21.
22. M.K. Gandhi, *Hind Swaraj or Indian Home Rule*, *op. cit.*, p. 54.
23. Mahadev Desai, "My Heart is in the Villages", *Harijan*, IV, No. 12 (May 2, 1936), p. 89.
24. Stephen R. Graubard, "An Interview with R.K. Narayan", *Daedalus*, 118, No.4 (Fall 1989), pp. 233-37.
25. Jawaharlal Nehru, *A Bunch of Old Letters*, *op. cit.*
26. M.K. Gandhi, "Untouchability", *Harijan*, I, No. 1 (February 11, 1933), pp. 4-5.
27. M.K. Gandhi, "Caste Corrosion", *Harijan*, X, No. 13 (May 5, 1946), p. 124.

Conclusion: Paradigms of Culture in Gandhi and Narayan

5

R.K. Narayan is a writer of realistic fiction and short stories. His realistic mode incorporates Gandhian thought. Like fiction, his non-fiction also shows the influence of Gandhian thought. The narrator in one of his short stories "A Breath of Lucifer" gives an account of Sam who develops an immoral relation with Marie and speaks contemptuously of almost all the women characters, namely Marie, the nurse and his own wife. The prologue to this story directly refers to Gandhi: "Mahatma Gandhi himself advised a youth whose heart was constantly agitated by the sight of women to walk with his eyes fixed on his toe, or on the stars above."[1] Besides, *The Painter of Signs* also stresses the observance of self-restraint in Gandhian context when Raman, obsessed with the thoughts of Daisy, attempts to shield himself against her charms, reflecting: Mahatma Gandhi had advised one of his followers in a similar situation, "Walk with your eyes fixed on your toes during the day, and on the stars at night" (*P.O.S.*, p. 40). Though Narayan's reference to Gandhi in the context of self-restraint sounds humorous, it reveals Narayan's awareness of Gandhi's thoughts on women.

Thus, the influence of Gandhian thought on R.K. Narayan's writing is quite clear. Gandhiji is not only an individual, but also a discourse. As a writer of the first generation of Indian English novelists, R.K. Narayan's fiction is obviously a part of Gandhian discourse, where it interacts with, or criticizes, or underlines Gandhian thoughts or the traditional cultural heritage in Indian context which is often quite available to Gandhian thoughts themselves.

Significantly, Narayan's fiction also accommodates the cultural debates in Gandhian context. These debates are about the medium of instruction, English versus Sanskrit and vernaculars, non-violence as a political policy, the use of khadi as an economic policy, village life versus city life and orthodox social conventions like untouchability and caste discrimination.

Of all the debates, the debate on the medium of instruction, acquires a central position in Narayan's fiction. English is viewed either as a colonial agency or a sign of progress and sophistication. *Swami and Friends* presents this debate through Swaminathan and the headmaster of the Board High School. Having been punished by the Headmaster of Albert Mission School, Swaminathan leaves it scornfully to join the Board High School with vernacular as medium. But once later the very sight of Albert Mission School fills him with love and nostalgia. The headmaster of the Board High School views Albert Mission School as 'pariah school'. Further, Raju's father in *The Guide* sends Raju to the old man's pyol school with vernacular as a medium and not to Albert Mission School even though the Albert Mission School is close by. But in *The World of Nagaraj*, Nagaraj, himself a product of English medium school, regards St. Stephen's as a good school. However, *A Tiger for Malgudi* presents this debate more precisely through the Captain, owner of Grand Malgudi Circus, and his wife: "You demanded that the boys should be sent to Lovedale School; that I have done, swallowing my own ideas at such a cost!" (*A.T.M.*, p. 37).

The linguistic debate in the contemporary India obsessed the minds of Indians considerably. People like Dr. Krishnadhan Ghosh attempted to popularize English language at the cost of native languages. Dr. Krishnadhan Ghosh developed an English ambience for his three children, including Sri Aurobindo even at home. Later he managed to admit them to the Loretto Convent School at Darjeeling, a school meant only for European children. Finally, he sent them to England. There he put them under the care of Mr. Drewett, Mrs. Drewett and Dr. Walker, the eminent British scholars, under strict instructions that his sons might not be allowed to mix up with any Indian or undergo any Indian influence. Consequently, Sri Aurobindo and his brothers were left ignorant of their mother-tongue. On the other hand, there were people like Gandhiji who objected to English simply because it prevented the growth of Indian vernaculars.

The World of Nagaraj presents linguistic debate and the harm done to Sanskrit by English. Nagaraj loves the English language. He proposes to write his book on Narada in English. His love for English leads him to fancy Sanskrit, the scriptural language of India, as a dead language. But the pundit, a Sanskrit scholar, lamenting the damage caused by English to Sanskrit, satirically remarks: "For Sanskrit studies our schools are unsuited; they are all right for English and other mlecha bashas" (*W.O.N.*, p. 97). Similary, Dr. Pal in *The Financial Expert* observes sadly that the books on Sociology are mostly written in English and not in the native languages.

This linguistic debate continues to persist in some other novels also. In *Waiting for the Mahatma* the character of Gandhi condemns English as a language of "our rulers" which has "enslaved us" (*W.F.M.*, p. 27). He addresses the people of Malgudi not in English but in Hindi. He even adds that he could speak to them in Tamil if he knew it. But in *The Bachelor of Arts* Mohan, a poet-student of Albert Mission College, writes his poems not in Tamil, his mother tongue, but in English.

However, the linguistic debate in contemporary India finds the best example in *A Tiger for Malgudi* through Captain, the owner of Grand Malgudi Circus, who delivers his message in three languages and explains:

> ...in Hindi since it is our national language and given to us by Mahatma Gandhi himself; also in English because as our beloved respected leader Nehru put it, it opens a window on the world. In Tamil, because it is, ah, our Mother Tongue, in which our greatest

> poets like Kamban and Valluvar composed; also the sublime inspiring patriotic songs of Bharathi, who can ever forget them? (*A.T.M.*, p. 66)

Though the Captain for his professional purpose attempts to harmonise English with Hindi and Tamil, he essentially reflects the linguistic debate in a historical sense.

Further, the Gandhian doctrine of non-violence invited various kinds of comments in contemporary India. Though Tilak and M.N. Roy criticized Gandhi's doctrine of non-violence, Einstein, Martin Luther King Jr., Pearl S. Buck, Jawaharlal Nehru and Dalai Lama interpreted it as a unique weapon to combat violence. *Waiting for the Mahatma* and *The Man-Eater of Malgudi* present this historical debate. *Waiting for the Mahatma* presents the disbelief in non-violence through Jagadish and Sriram. Jagadish, despite his use of khadi clothes and his earlier association with Gandhi, indulges in acts of violence which include setting of fire to the law courts, derailing, explosion of bomb. And Sriram's initiation into Gandhian philosophy and his later recourse to violent acts under the guidance of Jagadish imply the complexity of the principle of non-violence in a real historical sense.

The true faith in non-violence is exemplified through the character of Gandhi who appeals to everyone to practise absolute non-violence in thoughts, words and deeds. And later when communal violence takes place in East Bengal he walks through villages barefoot, speaks kindly to those involved in crimes, weeps for them and motivates them to swear never to indulge in violence again. Impressed by the message of non-violence, even the rowdy-looking men take "a vow of non-violence and a vow to protect the opposite faction" (*W.F.M.*, p. 244).

Similarly, *The Man-Eater of Malgudi* keeps alive the debate on non-violence prevalent in contemporary India through the violent Vasu on the one hand, and through Nataraj, Sastri and Rangi on the other, who always observe non-violence while dealing with Vasu.

Moreover, Gandhi's khadi scheme was recommended and popularized by a majority of Indian nationalists, namely

Dr. Rajendra Prasad, Vinoba Bhave, Jawaharlal Nehru and Kakasaheb Kalelkar. In *Waiting for the Mahatma* the character of Gandhi, Bharati and Sriram represent this class. The character of Gandhi regards khadi as a key to India's freedom. He spins everyday and urges Sriram to take a vow to wear only cloth made out of his own hands each day. Bharati propagates the mission of khadi and teaches spinning to Sriram. Following the call of the fictional Gandhi, Sriram spins yarn enough for his cloth. On the other hand, Ghanashyamdas Birla, a leading industrialist, objected to khadi in economic context stating that it yielded miserably low wages. This attitude to khadi also comes true in *The Vendor of Sweets* in terms of a considerably low wage that Jagan receives from spinning, though Jagan derives a spiritual joy in spinning and is thrilled while receiving his wages.

Further, Gandhian thought on machinery was also criticized by people like Nehru. Gandhiji objected to machinery because he believed that it would render millions of people unemployed. And Jawaharlal Nehru criticized Gandhi for taking the country to the bullock-cart age by rejecting machinery. This debate on machinery finds an apt example in *The Vendor of Sweets* in terms of Mali's unbridled passion for the story writing machine, juxtaposed by Jagan who is bewildered by Mali's scheme and distrusted it totally.

Like other issues the village-city issue also received a due attention in contemporary India. The rapid growth in science and technology led to an unprecedented growth in urbanization. And Gandhiji was against this urbanization. He not only preferred village-life to city-life, but also longed to go and settle himself in a village. He firmly believed that urbanization would completely rob the villages of their peace, culture and traditional crafts while the cities would breed in pollution, sin and such other vices. Gandhi's preference for the villages at the cost of cities is criticized by a majority of Indian nationalists like Gokhale, Tilak and Jawaharlal Nehru.

The village-city debate echoes itself in *The Bachelor of Arts*. Chandran after having experienced the harsh realities of city-life in Madras realizes: "The thought of Malgudi was very sweet" (*B.O.A.*, p. 102). Malgudi has always been treated as a village by Narayan. Chandran's encounter with Kailas in Madras and Kailas' attempt to divert Chandran to his own way, i.e. wine and prostitution, and the mechanical and impersonal people in Madras lead Chandran to realize: "There was no use remaining in the city any longer" (*B.O.A.*, p. 103). But Chandran's uncle seems to pour scorn on village-life and adore city-life. He believes that Malgudi would not lead Chandran "anywhere" and suggests to him "to go to a big city and see people" (*B.O.A.*, p. 52). Further, *The World of Nagaraj* also presents the village-city debate in terms of Tim's prejudice against village life, Nagaraj's openly expressed aversion to the smell of cattle and cattleshed, juxtaposed by Gopu's love for village life who dabbles in mud and manure like a baby.

Similarly, Gandhiji's fight against the evil of caste discrimination and untouchability brought a mixed response in an orthodox social milieu. It infuriated the orthodox Hindus but won the appreciation of the prominent nationalists like Rabindranath Tagore and Vinoba Bhave. *Waiting for the Mahatma* presents this debate precisely. The character of Gandhi appeals to the people to shun the evil of untouchability. In Mr. Natesh's house he makes a young untouchable boy to sit beside him on the divan, smooths out his matted hair with his fingers and speaks to him earnestly. Moreover, he visits the sweepers' colony and begins to stay there. While Mr. Natesh and Sriram's grandmother represent the class of the orthodox Hindus. Mr. Natesh's blood boils when the character of Gandhi calls for the untouchable boy: "Of course people must like poor people and so on, but why bring in such a dirty boy, an untouchable, up the steps and make him so important?" (*W.F.M.*, p. 48). And Sriram's grandmother adopts a bullying tone while addressing the scavenger who comes everyday to sweep the backyard of her house. She won't let the scavenger approach nearer than ten yards. Moreover, she also blames the character of Gandhi for bringing the "untouchables into the temples" (*W.F.M.*, p. 62).

The debate on untouchability and caste discrimination is available also in *The Guide*, *The Vendor of Sweets* and *The Painter of Signs*. In *The Guide* Raju's mother and maternal uncle, do not want to shelter Rosie because of her caste as a temple dancer. But Raju shelters Rosie and protests against his orthodox mother and maternal uncle. Similarly, in *The Vendor of Sweets* Jagan's sister and elder brother hate Jagan for sheltering Grace, a Christian girl, as a sister-in-law. But Mali and Jagan stay with Grace in their house, thus protesting against the evil practice of caste and untouchability. Similarly, in *The Painter of Signs* Raman's aunt protests against Raman's marriage with Daisy, considering Daisy to be a Christian, while Raman loves and marries Daisy eventually.

Thus, Raju's mother and maternal uncle, Jagan's sister and elder brother and Raman's aunt represent the class of orthodox Hindus, while Raju, Jagan, Mali and Raman represent the class of liberal and progressive people like Rabindranath Tagore and Vinoba Bhave.

The very application of Gandhian thoughts to R.K. Narayan's novels has brought forth many textual aspects which would otherwise remain ignored. For instance, the Gandhian thought on education in view of *The English Teacher* brings the headmaster, a minor character, who works on Gandhian lines, to the forefront. Krishnan's appreciation for the headmaster and his resignation from the Albert Mission College to join the headmaster's school just for one-fourth of his college salary, accord a higher degree of significance to the headmaster. The headmaster's stress on craft, observance of strict economy to maintain his school and the ample opportunity he allows the children to play, are in accordance with the Gandhian scheme of education. Thus, the Gandhian thought on education which received a considerable recognition in contemporary India, also finds an elaborate treatment in *The English Teacher* through the headmaster.

The Man-Eater of Malgudi contextualizes properly the Gandhian doctrine of non-violence through Sastri and Rangi, the minor characters, who consider non-violence as the best method to deal with the violent Vasu. Sastri is shocked to witness Vasu's maltreatment and cruelty. His sensitivity offends terribly as the stench of the carcasses dumped by Vasu on the attic of Nataraj's press pollutes the press and its surroundings. But he prefers to take a detached view. Considering Vasu's atrocity, Sastri likens him to Bhasmasura, a demon in Indian mythology, who having obtained a special boon from Lord Shiva, perpetrated destruction by placing his palms on the head of anyone he fancied to kill, but eventually reduced himself to ashes by unwittingly placing his palms on his own head. Sastri anticipates a similar end to Vasu also.

Similarly, Rangi's role is equally noteworthy. When everyone even the police inspector, fails to prevent Vasu from killing the temple elephant, Rangi takes up the lead, whispering seductively: "A woman in my position has her ways" (*M.O.M.*, p. 156). She takes a non-violent method to prevent Vasu by mixing some sleep-producing drug with Vasu's food hoping that Vasu would be in a stupor when the procession passes under his window that night. Tired and angry over many things and having broken the cot protected by mosquito net, Vasu orders Rangi to fan. He dozes off even without touching his food. Although, Rangi's idea to mix sleep-producing drug with Vasu's food doesn't seem to contribute directly to the elephant's safety, it enables Rangi to accompany Vasu that night, keep mosquitoes away by fanning for him thereby to let him doze off and allow the elephant pass unharmed under Vasu's window.

Thus, in the context of non-violence both Sastri and Rangi contribute to the thematic aspect of *The Man-Eater of Malgudi*. Rangi's positive role in the novel about saving the temple elephant may be in tune with her traditional role as a temple dancer.

Accordingly, the Gandhian doctrine of khadi allows Natesh and Jagadish, the minor characters in *Waiting for the Mahatma*, to represent the class of Indian people who used khadi deceitfully. Natesh uses khadi to impress the character of Gandhi without understanding the ethics of khadi. And Jagadish's use of khadi and his involvement in extremist activities themselves counter the values attached to khadi.

Similarly, the Gandhian doctrine of caste and untouchability accords a higher degree of significance to Mari and his wife Ponni, the minor characters in *The Dark Room*. Gandhiji emphatically argues that it is a sin to regard a man as untouchable on the basis of caste. He firmly believes that a man's status in society should be determined by his deeds and not by his birth.

The Dark Room validates this Gandhian postulate. Mari, the untouchable blacksmith who occasionally gives way to burglary, saves Savitri, a Brahmin woman, from committing suicide in the river at night. After having rescued Savitri, he leaves her on the river fearing that Savitri could identify him as a burglar. But troubled over the safety of Savitri, Mari comes back to see her next morning with his wife. Finding Savitri alone and helpless on the river, they request her to return to her husband. When Savitri strictly disagrees, they respectfully bring her to their village and offer her their best hospitality. Convinced of her own untouchability, Ponni hesitates to shelter Savitri. Thus, Mari and Ponni, the victims of caste discrimination, prove their nobility and reflect on the issue of untouchability.

Further, Narayan's religious faith in the context of Gandhian thought on religion acquires more authenticity. The psychic communion between Krishnan and his dead wife Susila in *The English Teacher* and a saint's philosophical discourse with a tiger on non-violence in *A Tiger for Malgudi*, seem to agree with the Gandhian belief. Gandhiji's belief in sin and chastisement, particularly with reference to the Bihar earthquake of 1934 echoes in *The Painter of Signs*. Gandhiji identifies the Bihar earthquake of 1934 with the sin of untouchability. And Daisy in *The Painter of Signs* interprets Raman's act of locking up his aunt's gods in a cupboard as effrontery.

Next, Gandhiji's belief that prayers, fastings and penances can bring miracle , also comes true in Narayan's novels. The prayers of Swaminathan and his grandmother in *Swami and Friends* bring Swaminathan, who had been lying nearly dead across the road in a distant highway, safely home. In *The*

Financial Expert Balu, Margayya's son, is a boon conferred upon Margayya as a fruit of his twelve-year prayers, including a pilgrimage to Thirupathi. And Margayya's prosperity itself is an outcome of a forty-day penance. Similarly, in *The Vendor of Sweets* the barrenness of Jagan's wife is cured by the worship of Santana Krishna on Badri Hill. However, the barrenness of Nagaraj's wife in *The World of Nagaraj* remains uncured despite a forty-day penance, special pujas and pilgrimages. But the novel justifies Sita's barrenness as a curse on her family, an ancestor having killed a King Cobra.

In fact, Gandhiji is essentially a practical reformer, a man of action. For him a theory stands validity only if it can be translated into action. He believes that a theoretical approach is enough to begin with. But the changes should be incorporated as per the exigencies of circumstances. Gandhiji presents the truth of human values. For him truth is experimental which is to be practised and not to be theorized. Truth is to be encountered and tested with fresh reality. Obviously, Gandhiji often modifies his statements though he is criticized for it. Gandhiji himself explains:

> At the time of writing I never think of what I have said before. My aim is not to be consistent with my previous statements on a given question, but to be consistent with truth as it may present itself to me at a given moment.[2]

As Gandhian thought presents experimental truth, Narayan's fiction also presents imaginative truth. The imaginary town of Malgudi which presents a fictional background to Narayan's novels is rightly viewed by G.J.V. Prasad as "less a place and more a point of view".[3] Though the topography of Malgudi also expands as Narayan's career as a novelist matures, Narayan is least concerned in presenting literal truth. C.N. Srinath is right to observe that Narayan gives "a mythical aura to factual details" to make Malgudi "a living reality in art".[4] Narayan himself explains:

> My fiction is set in my own background, though Malgudi is imaginary. Malgudi is fixed in the 1930s, and that gives me extraordinary freedom. I can even

> put a lighthouse there if I want to, though there is no coast near Malgudi.[5]

Thus, Narayan's novels are to be viewed as works of art which aim at imaginative truth, and not literal truth. Once replying to the charges of a research scholar who was aghast to find that streets change their locales without any apology in Narayan's books, Narayan makes it clear: "Malgudi is my imaginary town, what does it matter if Kabir Lane is here or Market Road there!"[6]

Swami and Friends presents an equivocal statement with reference to the number of schools in Malgudi which sounds like Gandhian view on machinery. At one instance, the novel mentions: "Albert Mission School is not the only school that this town, Malgudi, possesses" (*S.A.F.*, p. 7). This implies that there are plenty of schools in Malgudi. But at the other instance, the very statement counters itself when Swaminathan who left Albert Mission School to join the Board High School, resolves to leave the Board High School too, apprehends that he could then probably be sent to Trichinopoly or Madras because there are "no more schools in Malgudi" (*S.A.F.*, p. 145).

Similarly, *The Guide* (1958) at one instance in its narrative observes that Albert Mission College has "just been started at Malgudi" (*T.G.*, p. 48) whereas, Albert Mission College already figured much earlier in *The Bachelor of Arts* (1937). Besides, *Mr. Sampath: The Printer of Malgudi* (1949) observes: "The trains were passing Malgudi in an hour's time" (*M.S.P.M.*, p. 76) while *The Guide* (1958) records the service of 10.30 local, apart from "two whole trains each day, the noon train from Madras and the evening one from Trichy" (*T.G.*, p. 43). Moreover, *The Painter of Signs* (1977) observes Malgudi as a "conservative town unused to modern life" (*P.O.S.*, p. 146). While *Mr. Sampath: The Printer of Malgudi* (1949) describes Malgudi as if it had passed from "a semi-agricultural town to a semi-industrial town, with a sudden influx of population of all sorts" (*M.S.P.M.*, p. 26).

Humour and irony are the characteristic modes of modernity popularized by the West. Gandhiji is said to have acquired his sense of humour through his contacts with the West and the Western writers and thinkers. As a young boy Gandhiji exposes himself to modernity practically for the first time in England when he goes there to study for the law. Dazzled by the Western ways for quite some time, he begins to put on English clothes, imitate the manners and fashions of the English, spend a lot of money to make himself up and take lessons in dancing. After his return from England, Gandhiji has to leave for South Africa where he spends quite a few years.

Similarly, Narayan is directly exposed to the West through his reading of English literature and also through his visits to England which he makes occasionally either to see his friend Graham Greene or his publishers. Narayan's love for English literature is so deep that he wants to sustain it throughout his life. Narayan writes in English only because he cannot think of any other language to write in. English, he says, has helped him to express his thoughts admirably and perfectly. He considers English as the language of modern literature.

Gandhiji is essentially a man with a great sense of humour. Humour is not an additional gift to Gandhiji. It is the very blood that flows into his veins. His subtle humour makes him survive many personal and political crises. Gandhiji himself admits: "If I had no sense of humour, I would have long ago committed suicide."[7] Like Gandhiji Narayan also has a great sense of humour. As humour makes Gandhiji survive many personal and political crises, it also enables Narayan to bear the grief caused by the death of his young wife, Rajam. Narayan's writings bear a clear imprint of his cheerful personality. N. Ram aptly observes: "He indicates to us his pulse, and breaks into a typical R.K. Narayan smile—warm, teeming with life and a laidback expression, somewhat understated, like all his writing."[8]

Since humour is so fundamental both to Gandhiji and Narayan, a deeper probing into their comic mode may conveniently place them side by side. Their humour has a child-like innocence. It is capable of radiating joy and laughter all around. At times, humour becomes ironic. But it is always free from any malice or sarcasm.

Moreover, humour for Gandhiji is as important as his spinning or everyday prayer. Gandhiji would always prefer to spend his leisure hours playing, romping and cracking jokes with children. Amidst his numerous works and busy schedule, he would never forget to crack jokes. He could crack jokes even when he is engaged in serious political affairs. His speeches and writings also stress on humour. His autobiography and daily correspondence contain the finest gems of humour. Appreciating Gandhiji's sense of humour, Sarojini Naidu playfully called him "Mickey Mouse", one of the cartoons of Walt Disney. And George Bernard Shaw goes to the extent of saying that Gandhi is the only man in the East with a sense of humour. Jawaharlal Nehru in his autobiography comments:

> People who do not know Gandhiji personally and have only read his writings are apt to think that he is a priestly type, extremely puritanical, long-faced, Calvinistic, and a kill-joy, something like the "priests in black gowns walking their rounds". But his writings do him an injustice; he is far greater than what he writes, and it is not quite fair to quote what he has written and criticise it. He is the very opposite of the Calvinistic priestly type. His smile is delightful, his laughter infectious, and he radiates light-heartedness. There is something childlike about him which is full of charm. When he enters a room he brings a breath of fresh air with him which lightens the atmosphere.[9]

One may quote ample instances of humour from Gandhiji's life. Here are two famous examples. One day, while talking to Gandhiji, Louis Fischer, a well-known American writer, referred to President Roosevelt's Four Freedoms. Gandhiji humorously said, "Do your President's Four Freedoms include the freedom to be free?" This lively humour, though ironic, reveals Gandhiji's wit. Another example of humour can be quoted from Gandhiji's visit to the Buckingham Palace to see king George V and Queen Mary. Seeing Gandhiji in his loincloth, someone taunted whether Gandhiji wore enough clothes. Gandhiji quipped saying that the king had enough on for both of them. These two instances alone indicate the strength of Gandhiji's humour which, like non-violence, he also uses as a weapon.

It is observed that humour and irony are lacking in 19th and 20th century literatures written in Indian vernaculars. They are found more prominent in the writings of contemporary Indian writers writing in English. So, the influence of Western literature in terms of irony and humour on Indian writings in English is quite clear. Aliph Cheem's curious volume of poetry *Lays of Ind* (1875) which pictures 19th Century British life in India, is subtitled as "Comical, Satirical and Descriptive Poems Illustrative of English life in India." K. Chellappan observes that Narayan's novels portray "a two-tiered reality in which there is an intersection of modern time with mythical time, and their sense of comedy arises out of an interplay of a Western sense of comedy and a mythical sense of life as lila".[10]

Humour in Narayan's fiction does not allow a definite political commitment, and keeps a debate over an issue open. It provides a kind of critique of any system which may help that system to maintain its healthiness further. Significantly, Narayan keeps the existing social and political problems aside and concentrates largely on human characters. He delights in exposing those characters to an enjoyable and illuminating world.

Humour in Narayan's novels borders mainly on eccentricity of a character, comic scene, humorous dialogues and the tragic note facing life in its contradictions, and irony borders on exposure of folly, a situation and a tragic fate.

Humour in Narayan's novels largely arises out of eccentricity of their characters. *The Bachelor of Arts* presents Mr. Gajapathy, the Assistant Professor of English, who finds faults with Fowler's Modern English Usage, corrects everybody's English, while he himself reads Shakespeare in a sing-song fashion and with a vernacular twang. Ramani in *The Dark Room* is such an eccentric character. Himself an oppressor of his wife and a seducer of Shanta Bai, Ramani holds himself to ridicule while championing the cause of woman's equality: "It was all nonsense to keep men and women separate in water-tight compartments; women were as good as men and must be treated accordingly" (*D.R.*, p. 73). It is ironic too. And humour which arises out of the headmaster's eccentricity in *The English Teacher* considering books not for reading but doing a lot of private thinking, strikes a tragic note, for it underlines the tension between the headmaster and his wife.

Humour in *The Guide* takes an ironic twist. Raju's father sends Raju to an old teacher's school, primarily to prevent Raju from picking up and using the vulgar language of the railway trackmen. But humour arises when the old teacher himself turns out to be a very abusive man, who habitually addresses his pupils as donkeys and traces their genealogies on either side with thoroughness. Further, one can't hold back ones laughter to find Raju rejecting his traditional jibba and the lace-edged dhoti for dashing bush-shirts, corduroys, hair- and face-lotions and perfumes of all kinds to impress Rosie, Marco's wife. But the humour turns into irony of fate with Raju's realization that Rosie considers it better to end her life on Marco's doorsteps, rather than allowing herself to stand by Raju in his misfortune. And after Raju's release from jail humour also arises out of Raju's mistaken identity. Raju, the sinner, has to face life in its contradiction by acting as a saint. And the irony of fate strikes its note when Raju who initially thinks that the essence of sainthood lies "in one's ability to utter mystifying statements" has to go through prayers and fastings in order to become a true saint and a martyr (*T.G.*, p. 52).

Jagan in *The Vendor of Sweets* is perhaps the most comic creation. Himself a follower of Gandhi, Jagan exposes himself to mockery when he shows an excessive greed for wealth and an aversion to pay sales tax believing that Gandhi has made no reference to sales tax anywhere. The comic in Jagan is at its peak when in his final retreat Jagan goes into the forest carrying his check-book to see the goddess emerge from the stone. Srinivasa Iyengar ironically comments on Jagan's renunciation: "But at least the demon has been worsted, though the Deity hasn't arisen yet."[11]

Narayan's novels also abound in comic scenes. The scene in *Mr. Sampath: The Printer of Malgudi* is quite humorous in which the holy men with their foreheads stamped with ash and vermilion, reading some sacred texts, inaugurate Sampath's studio for the production of "The Burning of Kama" by sticking a string of jasmine and a dot of sandal paste on the camera. The camera, as Srinivas ironically remarks, becomes "their new god, who must be propitiated" (*M.S.P.M.*, p. 133). Here humour arises chiefly out of the tragic note, i.e. making fun of the Indian religious belief which also leads to the irony of fate when in the course of the rehearsal for the film, Ravi becomes mad and speechless, and Shanti, whose affairs with Sampath disrupt his family, escapes eventually leaving a note for Sampath: "If I find you pursuing me, I will shave off my head and fling away my jewellery and wear a white saree" (*M.S.P.M.*, p. 218). *A Tiger for Malgudi* presents an equally comic scene in which Raja, the tiger is evicted from the school. Besides, Raja's initiation into non-violence and philosophical discourse through the hermit are also comic.

It is true that Narayan does not deal much with the darker side of human existence. He is chiefly concerned with the portrayal of the average man, engrossed in the problems of everyday life. Narayan stares at those problems sympathetically with a ridiculing eye in such a way that the very problems become moral insights. The range of his characters includes students, teachers, painters, printers, family-planning workers, holy men, prostitutes, businessmen, moneylenders and sorcerers. One may occasionally find a rogue or an impostor. But there is complete absence of a murderer. Such characters make Malgudi teeming with life all the time. This may be one of the reasons for Narayan's humour. Natwar Singh observes:

> What appeals to me is the total absence of any kind of violence in his books. His men and women are God-fearing folk, they have no desire to shake the world nor to break each others' heads. They do love and

> hate, but as human beings and not as murderers. Sex they have too, but it is generally not allowed to get out of hand and the author never uses it as a prop to add spice to his narrative.[12]

Of all Narayan's characters, Vasu in *The Man-Eater of Malgudi* is alone presented as a stark villain. Though Vasu is a killer of wild animals, he never kills any human being. He bullies and browbeats people. The poet is scared of his presence. Sen, the journalist, cannot stand him even for a minute. Sastri always avoids his presence.

Naturally, the terror of Vasu doesn't allow Narayan's comic mode to operate so freely in *The Man-Eater of Malgudi.* Still the novel sustains humour. Introducing himself as a taxidermist to Nataraj, Vasu tells him that he has to be "where wild animals live". Nataraj adds, "And die". Nataraj's sense of humour makes Vasu laugh and admire Nataraj. But irony lies in the tragic fate of Vasu, the destroyer of animals, who meets his death eventually through mosquito, a tiny insect. Further, the encounter between Nataraj and the forest officer provides such a gentle humour. Worried over a considerable decrease in the number of wild animals when the forest officer with a view to gathering information from Nataraj in this respect asks him, "Where do they go?" Nataraj replies instantly, "Perhaps to other forests for a change." Nataraj's joke makes the forest officer laugh and he considers it as a good joke. Nataraj feels that "humour would establish a bond between us" (*M.O.M.*, p. 78).

The World of Nagaraj also presents humour in terms of Nagaraj's incapacity to retort Tim for taking liquor. Humour mingles with pathos as Nagaraj gently remarks: "I find some sort of smell when you pass, something like a spirit stove of a doctor's..." (*W.O.N.*, p. 60).

Narayan's humour is even capable of transcending the gloom in *The English Teacher* which is caused by the death of Krishnan's young wife, Susila. C.D. Narasimhaiah remarks that *The English Teacher* is "the farthest Narayan could go in the tragic mode".[13] The novel still sustains its comic propensity. For example, Krishnan's concern for the safe arrival of his wife and daughter while they are about to join him in Malgudi receives a comic portrayal. And later the description of the life after death dilutes the tragic note. The novel describes the life after death as ecstatic which is felt in the Divine Light flooding the spirits there, as the dead Susila tells Krishnan. Besides, the ample leisure, the freedom enjoyed by the spirits there, and then the music transporting the spirits to the higher planes, provide a great comic relief.

This presentation of life after death strikes humour also. As S.C. Harrex observes: "Even the 'great souls' or 'Helpers' of the after-life share Narayan's sense of humour, and they tell Krishnan, on one occasion when Susila is too convulsed with laughter to speak, that she said he should not take anything too tragically."[14] And again, towards the close of the novel humour arrives at its climax when Principal Brown expresses his doubt over Krishnan's ability to teach school children.

Narayan's comic mode allows an undercurrent of pain and anguish to run beneath it. N. Ram observes that Narayan's fiction is "distinctive for its voice, its fusion of the comic with the sad, and its philosophical depth".[15] And William Walsh also sums up Narayan's novels as "comedies of sadness".[16]

Humour takes a tragic note ironically in *Waiting for the Mahatma*. Sriram's initiation into Gandhian values, not on account of his love for those values but for Bharati, which sounds comic, eventually turns into pathos as Gandhi who is to bless Bharati and Sriram dies just a day before they are to marry.

Gandhian thought is largely an expression of the cultural heritage of India. And Narayan's novels are based on Indian myths. *The English Teacher* uses the Satyavan-Savitri myth. It presents the husband-wife relationship in a family. The myth assigns two different duties to Satyavan and Savitri. Satyavan carries firewood from the forest and Savitri devotes herself to the household duties. Gandhiji also considers man as a "bread-winner" and woman as a "keeper and distributor of the bread".[17]

The English Teacher presents Krishnan as a lecturer in Albert Mission College and Susila as a devoted housewife. The myth also presents love between Satyavan and Savitri through Savitri's penances to prevent Satyavan's death and also after Satyavan's death through her attempts to bring Satyavan back to life. And Gandhiji also expects infinite love between husband and wife. Gandhiji glorifies woman as the "incarnation of ahimsa".[18] He defines ahimsa as infinite love with infinite capacity for suffering. *The English Teacher* presents love between Krishnan and Susila through Krishnan's efforts to cure Susila from a fatal disease and also through his frantic efforts to establish a psychic communion between Susila and himself after Susila's death.

Similarly, *The Man-Eater of Malgudi* which is based on the Bhasmasura myth exemplifies that the evil has its own seeds of destruction. The myth describes at length how Bhasmasura after having won a special boon from Lord Shiva begins to destroy life on earth by placing his palm on the head of anyone he fancies to kill and how beguiled by Mohini, he reduces himself to ashes by placing his palm on his own head. And Gandhiji with his devout faith in scriptures believes that the "success of violence has been short-lived".[19] Gandhiji further observes that non-violence can "tame the wildest beast, certainly the wildest man".[20] *The Man-Eater of Malgudi* proves these beliefs true. Vasu, the oppressor of mankind and the destroyer of animals, who resolves to kill the temple elephant is tamed only by Rangi through her non-violent trick, and not by the police inspector.

The Gandhian non-violence in opposition to injustice, exploitation and terrorizing is viewed by Gunvant Shah as "Jatayu Vritti (Jatayu tendency)".[21] Jatayu in the *Ramayana* knows that he is not able to defeat Ravana. But he does not allow Ravana to kidnap Sita without any opposition. This Jatayu Vritti is found in Rangi in *The Man-Eater of Malgudi* who takes every possible measure to prevent Vasu from killing the elephant. However, the Jatayu Vritti is also noticeable in the people of Malgudi who take the elephant in a procession at night, quite unmindful of Vasu's threat. Thus, Rangi and the people of Malgudi present the traditional value. To quote Rumina Sethi: "Narayan's purpose in the novel is the protection of tradition in the form of the elephant which Vasu proposes to destroy in order to shock India into the twentieth century."[22]

Further, *The Painter of Signs* presents a modern version of the Santanu-Ganga myth in terms of the theme of birth and death. Gandhiji in *Self-Restraint v. Self-Indulgence* (1928) deals with birth control at length, advising "self-control as a means of attaining birth control".[23] But in *The Painter of Signs* Daisy propagates the killing of potential birth through contraceptives and abortions to curb the population growth of twentieth century India.

Gandhiji is both a man and an age. He follows Indian traditions and also strengthens them with modern spirit. R.K. Narayan, a writer of the first generation of Indian English novelists, lived in an Indian ambience which was charged invariably with Gandhian thoughts in the context of modernity. The stimulating Gandhian discourse, with its paradigms of Indian and Western cultures, becomes available to R.K. Narayan as a part of living conditions. Further, Gandhiji's thoughts often identify themselves with the Indian traditional values to the extent that both become inseparable from each other. R.K. Narayan as an author sensitively responds to it, amalgamating and discussing it to the degree an artist can do it.

NOTES

1. R.K. Narayan, *A Horse and Two Goats and Other Stories* (London: The Bodley Head Ltd., 1970), p. 121.
2. M.K. Gandhi, "Conundrums", *Harijan*, VII, No. 34 (September 30, 1939), pp. 288-89.
3. G.J.V. Prasad, "A Writer for all Time", *Biblio*, VI, Nos. 5 & 6 (May-June 2001), pp. 20-21.
4. C.N. Srinath, "R.K. Narayan's Comic Vision: Possibilities and Limitations", *World Literature Today*, 55, No. 3 (Summer 1981), pp. 416-19.
5. Stephen R. Graubard, "An Interview with R.K. Narayan", *Daedalus*, 118, No. 4 (Fall 1989), pp. 233-37.
6. G.J.V. Prasad, "A Writer for All Time", *op. cit.*
7. I.V. Chalapathi Rao, "Gandhi, the only Man in the East with a sense of Humour", *Triveni*, 68, No. 2 (April-June 1999), pp. 5-7.

8. N. Ram, "Return to Malgudi", *The Economic Times*, 2 October 1990, p. 5, cols. 1-5.
9. Jawaharlal Nehru, *Jawaharlal Nehru: An Autobiography* (1936; rpt. London: The Bodley Head, 1949), p. 515.
10. K. Chellappan, "The Dialectics of Myth and Irony in R.K. Narayan" in *R.K. Narayan: Critical Perspectives*, ed. A.L. McLeod (New Delhi: Sterling Publishers Pvt. Ltd., 1994), pp. 22-32.
11. K.R.S. Iyengar, *Indian Writing in English* (1984; rpt. New Delhi: Sterling Publisher Pvt. Ltd., 2005), p. 383.
12. Natwar Singh, "R.K. Narayan: The Creator of Sampat", *The Hindustan Times,* 9 April 1961, p. 2, cols. 2-5.
13. C.D. Narasimhaiah, *Essays in Commonwealth Literature: Heirloom of Multiple Heritage* (New Delhi: Pencraft International, 1995), p. 104.
14. S.C. Harrex, "R.K. Narayan's Grateful to Life and Death", *The Literary Criterion*, 8, No. 3 (Winter 1968), pp. 52-64.
15. N. Ram, "Malgudi's Creator: The Life and Art of R.K. Narayan", *Frontline*, 18, No. 11 (May 26 - June 8, 2001), pp. 4-12.
16. William Walsh, *R.K. Narayan: A Critical Appreciation* (New Delhi: Allied Publishers Pvt. Ltd., 1983), p. 7.
17. Nirmal Kumar Bose, *Selections from Gandhi* (Ahmedabad: Navajivan Publishing House, 1948), p. 240.
18. *Ibid.*, p. 241.
19. M.K. Gandhi, "What of the West?", *Young India*, VII, No. 36 (September 3, 1925), p. 304.
20. M.K. Gandhi, "Power of Ahimsa", *Young India*, XIII, No. 19 (May 7, 1931), p. 96.
21. Gunvant Shah, *Gandhi for the New Generation* (1982; rpt. Ahmedabad: Navajivan Publishing House, 1996), p. 16.
22. Rumina Sethi, "Inhabiting the Boundaries of the Nation-State: Locating 'Indianness' in Mulk Raj Anand and R.K. Narayan", *The Literary Criterion*, XLI, No. 1 (2006), pp. 55-68.
23. M.K. Gandhi, *Self-Restraint v. Self-Indulgence* (1928; rpt. Ahmedabad: Navajivan Publishing House, 1995), p. 111.

Select Bibliography

PRIMARY SOURCES

Narayan, R.K. *Swami and Friends*. 1935; rpt. Mysore: Indian Thought Publications, 2000.

——. *The Bachelor of Arts*. 1937; rpt. Mysore: Indian Thought Publications, 1995.

——. *The Dark Room*. 1938; rpt. Mysore: Indian Thought Publications, 1998.

——. *The English Teacher*. 1946; rpt. Mysore: Indian Thought Publications, 1996.

——. *Mr. Sampath: The Printer of Malgudi*. 1949; rpt. Mysore: Indian Thought Publications, 1998.

——. *The Financial Expert*. 1952; rpt. Mysore: Indian Thought Publications, 1994.

——. *Waiting for the Mahatma*. 1955; rpt. Mysore: Indian Thought Publications, 1993.

——. *The Guide*. 1958; rpt. Mysore: Indian Thought Publications, 1995.

——. *The Man-Eater of Malgudi*. 1961; rpt. Mysore: Indian Thought Publications, 1994.

——. *The Vendor of Sweets*. 1967; rpt. Mysore: Indian Thought Publications, 1992.

——. *The Painter of Signs*. 1977; rpt. Mysore: Indian Thought Publications, 1993.

——. *Talkative Man*. 1983; rpt. Mysore: Indian Thought Publications, 1996.

——. *A Tiger for Malgudi*. 1986; rpt. Mysore: Indian Thought Publications, 1999.

——. *The World of Nagaraj*. 1990; rpt. Mysore: Indian Thought Publications, 1999.

——. *Grandmother's Tale*. 1992; rpt. Mysore: Indian Thought Publications, 2000.

SECONDARY SOURCES

(A) Journals on Narayan

Batra, Shakti. "Impact of Gandhi on Indian Writing", *Indian Literature*. XVII, No. 3 (1974), pp. 38-51.

Cunningham, Valentine. "Baboo: *The Bachelor of Arts*, *The Dark Room* and *The English Teacher* by R.K. Narayan", *New Statesman*. 96, No. 2491 (15 Dec. 1978), pp. 829-30.

Gowda, H.H. Anniah. "Literary Criticism: R.K. Narayan", *The Literary Half-Yearly*. VI, No. 2 (July 1965), pp. 25-39.

Graubard, Stephen R. "An Interview with R.K. Narayan", *Daedalus*. 118, No. 4 (Fall 1989), pp. 233-37.

Harrex, S.C. "R.K. Narayan's Grateful to Life and Death", *The Literary Criterion*. 8, No. 3 (Winter 1968), pp. 52-64.

Mann, Charles W. "Narayan, R.K. Gods, Demons and Others", *Library Journal*. 89, No. 19 (November 1, 1964), p. 4359.

Narasimhaiah, C.D. "Makers of Indian English", *The Literary Criterion*. XXXIV, No. 1 (1999), pp. 5-32.

Pousse, Michel. "R.K. Narayan as a Gandhian Novelist", *The Literary Criterion*. XXV, No. 4 (1990), pp. 77-90.

Prasad, G.J.V. "A Writer for all Time", *Biblio*. VI, Nos. 5 & 6 (May-June 2001), pp. 20-21.

Ram, N. "Malgudi's Creator: The Life and Art of R.K. Narayan", *Frontline*. 18, No. 11 (May 26 - June 8, 2001), pp. 4-12.

Ranganath, N. "Realism in Literature: A Critique on R.K. Narayan's *The Guide*", *Triveni*. 48, No. 3 (Oct.-Dec. 1979), pp. 81-85.

Sarma, Renate. "Initiation and Quest—R.K. Narayan's *Waiting for the Mahatma*", *The Aligarh Journal of English Studies*. 20, No. 2 (1998), pp. 124-40.

Sethi, Rumina. "Inhabiting the Boundaries of the Nation-State: Locating 'Indianness' in Mulk Raj Anand and R.K. Narayan", *The Literary Criterion*. XLI, No. 1 (2006), pp. 55-68.

Srinath, C.N. "R.K. Narayan's Comic Vision: Possibilities and Limitations", *World Literature Today*. 55, No. 3 (Summer 1981), pp. 416-19.

Sundaram, P.S. "Naipaul on Narayan", *The Journal of English Studies*. 17 (1977), pp. 129-37.

Walsh, William. "Nataraja & the Packet of Saffron: The Indian Novel in English", *Encounter*. XXIII, No. 4 (October, 1964), pp. 78-83.

(B) Journals on Gandhi

Bhave, Vinoba. "Nai Talim", *Harijan*. XIII, No. 31 (Oct. 2, 1949), pp. 261-62.

——. "A Challenge to Sarvodaya Philosophy", *Harijan*. XIV, No. 15 (June 10, 1950), pp. 129-30.

Desai, Mahadev. "Weekly Letters", *Harijan*. IV, No. 7 (March 28, 1936), pp. 49-51.

——. "My Heart is in the Villages", *Harijan*. IV, No. 12 (May 2, 1936), p. 89.

——. "Prevention of Exploitation—Passive and Active". *Harijan*. IV, No. 29 (August 29, 1936), p. 226.

Gandhi, M.K. "Abusing the Khaddar", *Young India*. III, No. 6 (February 9, 1921), p. 41.

——. "National Education", *Young India*. III, No. 35 (September 1, 1921), pp. 276-77.

——. "What of the West?", *Young India*. VII, No. 36 (September 3, 1925), p. 304.

——. "My Kamadhenu", *Young India*. VIII, No. 20 (May 20, 1926), p. 187.

——. "My Conception of Patriotism", *Young India*. XI, No. 14 (April 4, 1929), pp. 107-08.

——. "Power of Ahimsa", *Young India*. XIII, No. 19 (May 7, 1931), p. 96.

——. "Christian Missions", *Young India*. XIII, No. 22 (May 28, 1931), pp. 121-22.

——. "Untouchability", *Harijan*. I, No. 1 (February 11, 1933), pp. 4-5.

——. "Bihar and Untouchability", *Harijan*. I, No. 52 (Feb. 2, 1934), p. 1.

——. "Village Tanning and Its Possibilities", *Harijan*. II, No. 30 (September 7, 1934), pp. 236-237.

——. "My Supposed Inconsistency", *Harijan*. II, No. 39 (November 9, 1934), p. 308.

——. "Mission of Khadi", *Harijan*. III, No. 21 (July 6, 1935), p. 164.

——. "Fallacies", *Harijan*. III, No. 31 (September 14, 1935), p. 244.

——. "Is Khadi Economically Sound?", *Harijan*. IV, No. 19 (June 20, 1936), p. 145.

——. "A Humble Villager of Birbhum", *Harijan*. IV, No. 48 (January 9, 1937), p. 383.

——. "Criticism Answered", *Harijan*. V, No. 25 (July 31, 1937), pp. 196-98.

——. "Higher Education", *Harijan*. VI, No. 22 (July 9, 1938), pp. 176-78.

——. "Conundrums", *Harijan*. VII, No. 34 (September 30, 1939), pp. 288-89.

——. "Is Congress a Hindu Organisation?", *Harijan*. VII, No. 41 (November 18, 1939), pp. 341-43.

——. "What is Woman's Role?", *Harijan*. VIII, No. 2 (February 24, 1940), pp. 12-14.

——. "Caste Corrosion", *Harijan*. X, No. 13 (May 5, 1946), p. 124.

Mashruwala, K.G. "The Sarvodaya Conference—II", *Harijan.* XIII, No. 4 (March 27, 1949), pp. 28-29.

Pyarelal. "Limits of Industrialization", *Harijan.* VI, No. 51 (January 28, 1939), pp. 438-39.

Rao, I.V. Chalapathi. "Gandhi, the Only Man in the East with a Sense of Humour", *Triveni.* 68, No. 2 (April-June 1999), pp. 5-7.

(C) Newspapers

Barr, Donald. "A Man Called Vasu: The Man-Eater of Malgudi by R.K. Narayan", *New York Times.* 12 Feb. 1961, p. 5, cols. 1-2, p. 16, col. 4.

Joshi, Rita. "Vintage Narayan", *The Hindustan Times.* 22 July 1990, p. 4, cols. 6-8.

Karnani, Chetan. "Critique of an Author: The Paradox of R. K. Narayan", *The Times of India.* Dec. 22, 1968, p. 10, cols. 2-4.

Narayan, R.K. "English in India: Process of Transmutation", *The Times of India.* 3 December 1964, p. 8, cols. 3-5, p. 9, col. 5.

Ram, N. "Return to Malgudi", *The Economic Times.* 2 October 1990, p. 5, cols. 1-5.

Singh, Natwar. "R.K. Narayan: The Creator of Sampat", *The Hindustan Times.* 9 April 1961, p. 2, cols. 2-5.

(D) Books on R.K. Narayan

Alam, Fakrul. "Narrative Strategies in Two Narayan Novels" in *R.K. Narayan: Critical Perspectives*, ed. A.L. McLeod. New Delhi: Sterling Publishers Pvt. Ltd., 1994.

Chellappan, K. "The Dialectics of Myth and Irony in R.K. Narayan" in *R.K. Narayan: Critical Perspectives,* ed. A.L. McLeod. New Delhi: Sterling Publishers Pvt. Ltd., 1994.

Girla, Shiv K. *R.K. Narayan: His World and His Art.* Meerut: Saru Publishing House, 1984.

Iyengar, K.R.S. *Indian Writing in English.* 1984; rpt. New Delhi: Sterling Publishers Pvt. Ltd., 2005.

Jha, Rama. *Gandhian Thought and Indo-Anglian Novelists.* Delhi: Chanakya Publications, 1983.

Naik, M.K. *Dimensions of Indian English Literature.* New Delhi: Sterling Publishers Pvt. Ltd., 1984.

Narasimhaiah, C.D. *Essays in Commonwealth Literature: Heirloom of Multiple Heritage.* New Delhi: Pencraft International, 1995.

Narayan, R.K. *A Horse and Two Goats and Other Stories.* London: The Bodley Head Ltd. 1970.

——. *My Days.* Delhi: Orient Paperbacks, 1986.

Pathan, B.A. *Gandhian Myth in English Literature in India.* New Delhi: Deep & Deep Publications, 1987.

Walsh, William. *R.K. Narayan: A Critical Appreciation.* New Delhi: Allied Publishers Pvt. Ltd., 1983.

(E) Books on Culture & Gandhi

Anand, Mulk Raj. *On Education.* Bombay: Hind Kitabs Ltd., 1947.

——. "Why I Write?" in *Perspectives on Mulk Raj Anand,* ed. K. K. Sharma. Ghaziabad: Vimal Prakashan, 1978.

Anderson, Benedict. *Imagined Communities: Reflections on the Origin and Spread of Nationalism*, 1983. rpt. London: Verso, 1991.

Bhabha, Homi K. "Introduction: Narrating the Nation", in *Nation and Narration*, ed. Homi K. Bhabha. London: Routledge, 1990.

Bose, Nirmal Kumar. *Selections from Gandhi.* Ahmedabad: Navajivan Publishing House, 1948.

Bowle, John. *The Nationalist Idea.* London: Ampersand Ltd., 1955.

Chatterjee, Partha. *Nationalist Thought and the Colonial World: A Derivative Discourse?* Delhi: Oxford Univ. Press, 1986.

Das, Chittaranjan. "Bengal and the Bengalees" in *Chittaranjan Das: A Biography of His Vision and Ideas*, ed. Verinder Grover. New Delhi: Deep & Deep Publications, 1998.

Easwaran, Eknath. *Gandhi the Man*. Northamptonshire: Turnstone Press Ltd., 1983.

Einstein, Albert. "On Peace—and Gandhi" in *Profiles of Gandhi*, ed. Norman Cousins. Delhi: Indian Book Company, 1969.

Friedman, Jonathan. *Cultural Identity and Global Process*. London: Sage Publications, 1994.

Gandhi, M.K. *An Autobiography or the Story of My Experiments with Truth*. 1927; rpt. Ahmedabad: Navajivan Publishing House, 2004.

——. *Self-Restraint v. Self-Indulgence*. 1928; rpt. Ahmedabad: Navajivan Publishing House, 1995.

——. *Hind Swaraj or Indian Home Rule*. 1938; rpt. Ahmedabad: Navajivan Publishing House, 2000.

——. *Constructive Programme: Its Meaning and Place*. 1941; rpt. Ahmedabad: Navajivan Publishing House, 2003.

——. *Basic Education*. 1951; rpt. Ahmedabad: Navajivan Publishing House, 1962.

——. *The Problem of Education*. Ahmedabad: Navajivan Publishing House, 1962.

Kluckhohn, Clyde. *Culture and Behavior*. 1962; rpt. New York: The Free Press of Glencoe, 1964.

Kripalani, Krishna. "Modern Literature" in *A Cultural History of India*, ed. A.L. Basham. Oxford: Clarendon Press, 1975.

Mehta, Hansa. *Indian Woman*. Delhi: Butala & Company, 1981.

Nandy, Ashis. *The Illegitimacy of Nationalism: Rabindranath Tagore and the Politics of Self*. Delhi: Oxford University Press, 1994.

Nehru, Jawaharlal. *Jawaharlal Nehru: An Autobiography*. 1936; rpt. London: The Bodley Head, 1949.

——. *A Bunch of Old Letters*. 1958; rpt. Bombay: Asia Publishing House, 1960.

Nirvedananda, Swami. *Swami Vivekananda on India and Her Problems*. Calcutta: Advaita Ashram, 1995.

Parekh, Bhikhu. *Gandhi: A Very Short Introduction*. New York: Oxford University Press Inc., 2001.

Plamenatz, John. "Two Types of Nationalism" in *Nationalism: The Nature and Evolution of an Idea*, ed. Eugene Kamenka. London: Edward Arnold Ltd., 1976.

Premchand, Shivrani Devi. *Premchand Ghar Mei*. Delhi: Atmaram & Sons, 1991.

Radhakrishnan, S. *Freedom and Culture*. Madras: G.A. Natesan & Co., 1936.

Rai, Lajpat. *Young India: An Interpretation and A History of the Nationalist Movement from Within*. 1916; rpt. Delhi: Publications Division, Ministry of Information and Broadcasting, Govt. of India, 1968.

Renan, Ernest. "What is a Nation?" in *Nation and Narration*, ed. Homi K. Bhabha. London: Routledge, 1990.

Saiyidain, K.G. *Significance of Gandhi as a Man and Thinker*. 1970; rpt. New Delhi: Publications Division, Ministry of Information and Broadcasting Govt. of India, 1994.

Sarma, D.S. "The Father of the Nation" in *Problems in Asian Civilizations: Gandhi Maker of Modern India?*, ed. Martin Deming Lewis Massachusetts: D.C. Heath and Company, 1965.

Shah, Gunvant. *Gandhi for the New Generation*. 1982; rpt. Ahmedabad: Navajivan Publishing House, 1996.

Singh, B.P. *India's Culture: The State, the Arts and Beyond*. New Delhi: Oxford University Press, 1998.

Sinha, B.P. *Social and Political Concern in the Novels of Nayantara Sahgal*. Jaipur: Book Enclave, 2001.

Spear, Percival. *The Oxford History of Modern India (1740-1947)*. London: Oxford University Press, 1965.

Tagore, Rabindranath. *The Centre of Indian Culture*. Madras: The Society for the Promotion of National Education, 1919.

Tylor, Edward B. *Primitive Culture: Researches into the Development of Mythology, Philosophy, Religion,*

Language, Art and Custom. Vol. I. London: Garden City Press Ltd., 1913.

Vireswarananda, Swami. *The Complete Works of Swami Vivekananda*. Vol. III. Almora: Advaita Ashrama, 1932.

Vivekananda, Swami. *The Complete Works of Swami Vivekananda*. Vol. III. Almora: Advaita Ashram, 1932.

Index